Sewing Tales

TO *Stitch* AND *Love*

18 toy patterns
for the storytelling sewist

Kerry Goulder

KP CRAFT
Cincinnati, Ohio

Table of Contents

1

In the Forest ~ 18

2

Coastal Waters ~ 44

3

Arctic Adventures ~ 70

4

A Rainy Day ~ 92

Foreword

As makers, crafters and stitchers, some projects we make are for the moment, a temporary escape into our imaginations. Other projects are an investment in the future. And then there are those magical projects that are both; they lead us down paths of fancy and result in treasured heirlooms that will inspire and delight generations to come.

In *Sewing Tales to Stitch and Love*, Kerry Goulder brings us eighteen lovingly-crafted projects that are not only fun to make, but will prompt years of creative play. To kick-start our imaginations, each project is tied to a charming story, leading us from a whimsical woodland to the coastal waters, the Arctic, and back.

With a rare talent for three-dimensional design, Kerry has honed and sculpted patterns from gnomes, mushrooms and mice to turtles, orcas and igloos, sharing each of these patterns with us in one tidy book.

Treat yourself to a sweet escape. Whether sewing for yourself or a loved one, *Sewing Tales* provides a rich trove of enduring keepsakes to create and treasure. Kerry's endearing stories reflect the warmth and bright imagination with which this book was thoughtfully fashioned. Build your cast of characters and let Kerry's stories send you and your loved ones on a memorable adventure together.

Love,
Heather Bailey

World-renowned textile and product designer Heather Bailey has a soft spot for softies. She began sewing and designing dolls as a young child, and today publishes a wide range of popular sewing patterns, from toys to handbags. Her patterns and fabrics are in fabric stores worldwide, and her widely-read blog can be found at HELLOmynameisHeather.com.

Come, let me tell you a story.

The ideas in this book have come from many places in my life. Some are gifts that I have made for friends and family, like the tote bag I first made for a dear friend and then as Christmas presents for many of my daughters' teachers. The turtle was designed in my head while on a five-hour drive heading home, to submit for a fabric contest many years ago. The lightbulb was a class project from my college days. All the animals pay homage to my own daughters, who love animals with a passion. The gnomes, which really started the whole concept of this book, come from a lifetime obsession my twin sister and I have had with fairies and gnomes.

I am excited to share many stories from my life, tucked within the pages of this book. All of the project stories are fictional, but for fun I have stirred in a little dash of reality here and there. When I was younger, my paternal grandfather actually had a boat named Water Baby docked in Maryland. My mom's brother Bob loved swimming out in Greenport, New York, where my Granny and Grandpop lived for many years. Naturally, Uncle Bob's name was perfect for the buoy project!

Each of these patterns tells its own story. Each one holds a thought, an idea, a dream, or even a memory that is very special to me. I hope that as you explore this book and create any one of these projects, or all of them, that it will do the same for you. May these pages help you channel your inner sewist and spark your imagination to write your own story or two.

TOOLS

1. Rotary blades are used to cut straight edges quickly and accurately. You'll need a **straightedge** or **acrylic ruler** and a good **rotary cutting mat** also.

2. Dress cutting shears are used primarily for cutting patterns that are laying flat on a table. The blades are straight-edged, but the handles are set at an angle.

3. Fine-tip scissors are best for cutting small details in small spaces. These are also good to have for cutting thread ends.

4. Spring-action snips or **clipping scissors** are the best for clipping and notching edges. The grip handles and spring action help to prevent your hands from tiring too quickly, as they spring open after each cut. I'll never go back to using regular scissors for clipping and notching my edges!

5. Pinking shears are scissors with zigzag blades and are used to prevent the edges of your materials from fraying. They also help to reduce bulk. Use these if the raw edge will remain exposed or if you want to reduce the bulkiness of your seam edge.

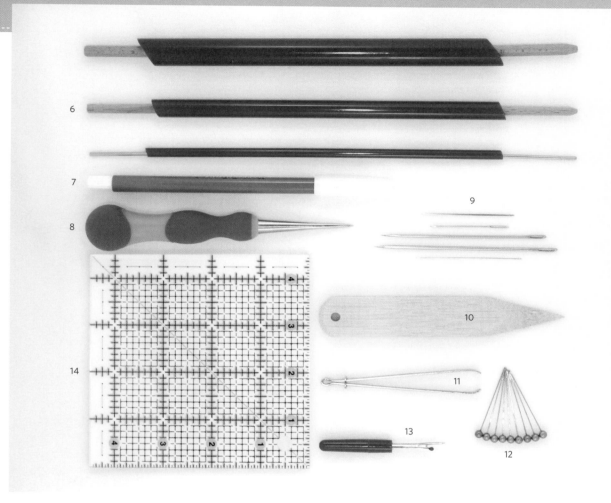

6. Turning tools come in various sizes. The three needed for the projects in this book (and most commonly found as a set) are ½" (1.3cm), ⅜" (10mm) and ¼" (6mm). Turning tools will help you turn all the arms, legs and other small or narrow pieces right-side-out. This is a purchase worth every penny.

7. Fabric marker/marking pens are usually water-soluble, but can also be a type of disappearing ink. Fabric markers are useful for marking centers, fold measurements, connecting points or eye locations.

8. Awls are used to pierce holes in fabrics, typically thick leather, but also multiple layers of fabric. The awl will be helpful for the *Adventurer's Backpack* (see page 32), but you can also use eyelet pliers (not shown).

9. Using the right **needles** for your projects will ensure the best results. Standard needles are used for closing up after stuffing. Beading needles are helpful when sewing bead eyes on dolls and stuffies because their smaller "eyes" pass through the bead holes easier. Doll needles are good for adding embroidery eyes and also for passing thread through a very thick section because they are longer than normal and very durable. Since they are thicker than the average needle, they can create large holes in your fabric, so use them gently.

10. A **bamboo point turner** helps to poke the corners out of your projects. When you are wanting to press center points to line up fabrics easily, this tool can also serve as a little press to create the crease, instead of your nails or a pencil. This is one of the cheapest and most convenient tools you can get.

11. Fabric tweezers (also known as a *bodkin*) are one of my favorite tools. These are great for pulling elastic through tubes and tunnels, and grabbing small pieces of fabric when your fingers can't do the job.

12. Pins come in many shapes and sizes. For all of these projects, I have used standard ball-tipped straight pins that come in a reusable container.

13. Seam rippers are used for all those little mistakes that are bound to happen. I have more than one, as they are so helpful.

14. Straightedges come in many shapes, sizes and lengths. For some of the projects in this book, you will need a rectangular straightedge at least 24" (61cm) long. Other projects may only need a smaller straightedge. If you start with the longest one, you can get smaller rulers later as desired, but they are not necessary right away.

15. (Not shown) Unless you will sew all of your projects by hand, you will need a **basic sewing machine** with a standard foot, though a zigzag foot for the gnome boots is handy. I'm the first to admit that I am zipper-and-buttonhole phobic, so I try not to design patterns that require these machine feet.

16. (Not shown) There are a few **seam sealants** on the market, such as Fray Block, that help to prevent your fabric edges from fraying while being handled. Be sure to follow the manufacturer's instructions and test first on a small scrap of your fabric before using on your finished project.

MATERIALS

Sherpa suede (A) is a very soft, fuzzy fabric on one side and a soft, smooth, suedelike fabric on the other. This fabric is used for the gnome boots, but can also be used for the polar cubs and so much more. Be sure to vacuum your machine when you are done using it to prevent any clogging from all the loose fibers.

Quilter's cotton (B) is my hands-down favorite fabric. I rarely use anything else. It comes in the most beautiful prints and solids, is easy to use, washes well and is soft to the touch. If I am making dolls or stuffies for gifts, I prewash my fabrics with like colors in cold water, using a gentle detergent.

Low-loft cotton batting (C) is best used between two fabric layers for quilting. I prefer to use natural cotton instead of poly battings on tote bags and the *Dolly Moses Basket* set, since it requires less quilting." Scraps can be shredded and used for stuffing.

Pre-quilted fabrics (D) are great for making tote bags. You can buy them single-faced (one side is fabric, the other side is batting) or double-faced (the batting is quilted between two layers of fabric). If you have a favorite fabric, you can quilt your own. The more it is quilted the sturdier it is, but this type of fabric will still relax over time without the use of stabilizers.

Corduroy (E) is a ribbed fabric that I used for making the *Adventurer's Backpack* (page 32). You can buy new, but you can also use recycled materials for the backpack, including corduroy from an old pair of pants. In fact, using any sturdy recycled fabric, even worn denim jeans, can make a great keepsake.

Muslin is a lighter weight fabric than a quilter's cotton. It is best used for testing a pattern you are making for the first time. If you are learning how to sew or trying a pattern for the first time, muslin is a much cheaper alternative to use before cutting into your awesome (expensive) fabric.

For **stuffing**, we all have our preferences, but there are a few options to consider. Poly fillers are most commonly available and give stuffed toys a lightweight feel. Prices vary; cheaper versions can clump, while the more expensive kinds can be very silky and smooth. If you'd like to go the natural route, you can use a dense bamboo, which offers a very old-school feel. Because the bamboo is thicker, it will take much longer to dry than a poly filling.

Stabilizers come in various thicknesses for different project needs. These are good for providing stiffness and durability.

Pattern paper is a nonwoven tracing fabric that is great for cutting out pattern pieces, which can then be stored and used over and over. It is thin enough to see through, but thick enough to not tear too easily. Create-A-Pattern by Bosal is available on a large roll and works great!

Yarn will only be needed for the gnome doll hair and optional scarves. You can use any kind you'd like, but if you plan to wash the doll, or think you may need to, I would not recommend wool as it will shrink in the wash. If you want more strands, I would use a thinner or standard weight, and nothing too thick.

Tip To save cutting time, trace the pattern templates onto pattern paper, lay onto the fabric (matching stretch direction) and pin in place. Cut out each fabric pattern piece and the pattern paper at the same time, then unpin.

Embroidery floss is best for making eyes on stuffies that are potential gifts for babies or young children. You can use a basic six-strand cotton floss, or you can upgrade to a pure silk floss.

Not all **sewing threads** are equal. Be kind to your machine and your projects, and use a good thread. I most often use an all-purpose, 100-percent polyester thread. I prefer to use white with the lighter fabrics but will switch to a darker color for darker fabrics when the need arises. You can also match your threads to your fabrics, if you want.

Basic techniques and stitches

Strip-piecing

Hems

A **back stitch** or **lock stitch** locks in the stitches at the beginning and the end of the seam to secure the ends, as if you made a knot. *This step is very important when making anything you are turning right side out.* If the seam is not locked, it will unravel and the fabric pieces will not stay connected the way they need to be.

A **blanket stitch** can be used to protect fabric edges from unraveling and to add a decorative stitch to attach the patches on *Drifter the Orca Whale* (page 82). To make a blanket stitch (following the labeled photograph below), pull your threaded needle up at A, down at B and up at C, with the thread looped under the needle, and pull through. Watch your spacing and be sure to tighten the stitches equally as you go, for a neat and uniform look.

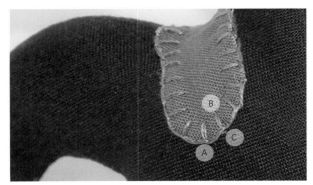

Blanket stitch

A **top stitch** is a stitch added near a folded seam edge for decorative purposes or to connect more than one layer of fabric. It can be ⅛" (3mm) away from the folded edge or ½" (1.3cm) away, depending on the needs of the pattern or the look that is desired.

Strip-piecing involves continuously stitching from one piece of material to the next. Instead of stopping to lift the foot and clip the threads, you stitch all the way through one piece and then immediately start sewing on another piece. The pieces are loosely connected until they are clipped apart. If the pieces are being turned right side out, they will still require a back stitch added at the beginning and end of each unit.

A **single hem** is a raw edge that is folded down once so that wrong sides are facing. Although the raw edge is facing inward and has been sewn, it is still visible. This type of hemming is used when the raw edge has been serged or will be hidden from view, as on the top rim of the *Ready, Sew & Go Tote Bag* (page 99).

A **double hem** is a raw edge that is folded twice, once as a single hem and then one more time, so the raw edge is no longer visible and there is a top and bottom fold along the hem. Use a double hem when the edge needs to be protected from unraveling. The *Adventurer's Backpack* pockets are double-hemmed for protection. Double hemming also adds bulk to side seams.

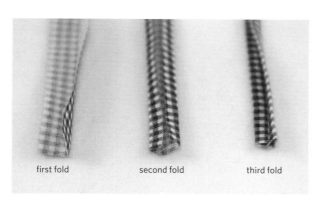

first fold second fold third fold

Folding sequence for binding

Curves and corners clipped and notched.

Inset seams or set-in seams are not as difficult as they sound. It is simply a matter of not starting the stitch at the edge perpendicular to the seam, but instead starting ¼" (6mm) or ½" (1.3cm)—a seam allowance's width—away from that edge. This process is used when making the *Adventurer's Backpack* (page 32) and the *Mimi the Hot-Air Balloon* (page 85) basket.

You will need to **make binding** for the gnome doll overalls and the *Adventurer's Backpack*. The steps are: (1) Fold and press the binding fabric strip in half length-wise, wrong sides facing; (2) Open the strip and fold each side halfway so the raw edges meet in the center fold, then press lightly; (3) Fold it in half again (where that first center line is) and press one last time; (4) Top stitch the two folds together.

Not clipping and notching will result in rough, mis-shapen edges.

Clipping and notching curves and corners is time-consuming but important to do, so that your fabric isn't too tight along the sewn edges and doesn't appear misshapen once stuffed. After clipping and notching, the fabric will look smoother along all the edges once stuffed.

Inward curves require a ¼" (6mm) straight clip along the edge of the seam, and an outward curve requires a small triangular notch along the outside edge. When clipping and notching, there is a fine balance between cutting the fabric edge and how close you can get to the seam, without the fabric ripping under stress once stuffed. Use caution and leave a little room, with at least three to four threads unclipped.

Curved seams lay nicer and smoother if clipped and notched first.

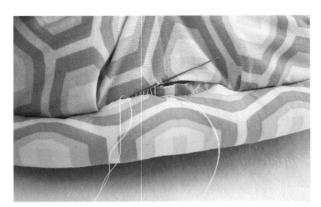

Ladder stitch

Fussy cutting means to be particular with what part of a fabric you want to cut for your pattern piece. Fussy cutting allows you to maximize the repeat effect of a pattern and it allows you to use specific elements within the fabric pattern. When you fussy cut, realize that you will need more fabric than the pattern calls for, depending on the size of the repeat.

Ladder stitch is the hand stitch I use most often to close stuffed projects. It looks just like a ladder as you place the needle in one side, laterally along the fold, cross over the gap, and through the other side laterally in the same direction. (Knot your thread prior to starting.) You continue all the way down, pulling the thread gently to close the gap as you go. Knot the end and tuck the needle and the end of the thread through the fabric and out a random area, and clip. If you cut near the knot, the thread and seam are more likely to come undone. The needle and thread should be tucked at least 1" (2.5cm) away from the seam edge to prevent this.

Knife pleats are folds in the fabric that are laid to one side and look like blades of a knife when standing up. They are typically equal in length and have a 3:1 ratio—for every 3" (7.6cm) of fabric, you get a 1" (2.5cm) pleat.

Box pleats are a series of folds in the fabric that when pulled apart have a box shape. Box pleats also have a 3:1 ratio, but are different in that the top of the fold is 1" (2.5cm), and the sides are only ½" (1.3cm) and meet in the middle, underneath the 1" (2.5cm) box top.

Knife pleats

Box pleats

TO FINISH A QUILT WITH A SIMPLE ROLLED EDGE

You can finish a basic blanket or quilt in a number of ways. For the quickest method, you can simply sew both sides right sides together, turn right side out, and top stitch all the way around. You can also bind the quilt using binding you've made or bought premade, which will take more time. A simple rolled edge is prettier than the top stitch and less work than the binding, but gives the same look as binding on the front side.

You can use this simple rolled-edge method for your *Dolly Moses Basket* blanket (page 94).

1. Place the quilt back on the table right side down, with the batting and then the quilt top right side up on top. The quilt back should be at least ½" to ⅝" (1.3cm to 1.6cm) larger on all sides, unless you are going to use a binding method (not shown).

Fold each corner of the quilt back diagonally, up to the tip of the corner of the quilt top.

2. Fold each quilt-back corner up again and pin in place.

4. Fold the edges again, up and over the quilt top and pin in place.

3. Fold the sides in half so the raw edge of the backing meets the raw edges of the batting and quilt top.

5. Top stitch the inside fold all the way around the blanket.

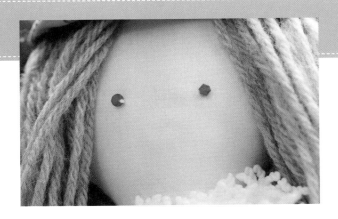

TO SEW BEAD EYES

As the old proverb says, "Eyes are windows to the soul." When your dolls or stuffies need their eyes to see, choose them wisely. I love using 4mm bicone crystal beads for gnome doll eyes so they sparkle in the day and twinkle at night.

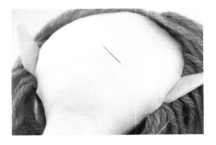

1. Mark where you want the eyes to be placed using a washable fabric marker or disappearing marker. Using a threaded beading needle, place a knot in the end of the thread and place the needle through the side seam of the head under the ear and direct it out to the first mark for one of the eyes.

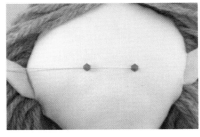

2. Place two beads on the thread and needle to make sure those are the colors you like, and that you've got the right placement.

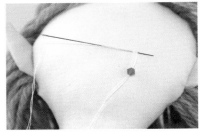

3. Take one bead off and place the needle through the fabric within ⅛" (3mm) of the thread coming out of the fabric.

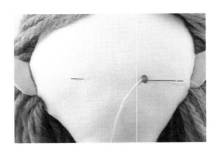

4. Continue to loop the thread through the bead and the fabric in the same direction, at least three times. After the third time, place the needle through the fabric under the eye, and direct it out from the other mark for the second eye.

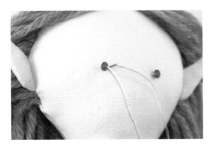

5. Loop the needle and thread through the bead and fabric at least three times on this side, repeating step 4.

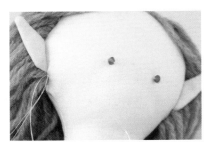

6. Once completed, place the needle through the fabric under the eye, and direct it out through the opposite side seam from where the thread went in. Loop the thread into a secure knot and direct the needle back through the fabric and out the back of the neck, then clip the thread end.

TO SEW EMBROIDERY EYES

When deciding what type of eyes to add, consider the safety and simplicity of embroidery knotted eyes. Embroidery knots for eyes on items intended for small children are ideal, as they are not a choking hazard.

You'll need a standard six-strand, 12" (30.5cm) piece of embroidery floss for each doll or stuffie.

1. Push a threaded doll needle into one side of the head, making sure it's level horizontally and vertically when exiting the other side.

2. Pull it through the other side, leave some floss hanging, and put it back through again.

3. Cut the floss on the looped side so you have two separate pieces on both sides. Tie a knot on each side, pulling tighter each time.

4. On one side, hold both pieces together and tie another knot. Before pulling tight, grab the knot that is already there and guide the floss to to tie underneath the knot you are holding. Do this a couple of times, and then repeat this for the other side.

5. Using the doll needle again, thread the floss through the eyes and out the opposite side of the head. This will prevent the eyes from coming undone over time.

6. Carefully trim the ends off without cutting into the fabric.

1

In the Forest

I may not be a little girl anymore with pigtails in my hair, but I will always believe that these sweet gnomes really exist in some far-off, enchanted little world. Now my girls do, too. Do you?

The Gnomes: PIPER & SAGE

Deep in the valley of Franconia, the hobble-bush grows in large canopies that cover the valley floor. As people walk the trails, they never seem to notice the little gnomes that live in the roots of nearby trees. If you look closely, though, you just might see these two.

Piper loves to draw and doesn't go anywhere without a pad of paper and her pencils. She draws pictures of her friends and family and lots of animals, and she even designs new houses for the gnomes. She also tends to all the pets and helps them get well when they are sick. Her younger sister Sage giggles a lot and hugs everyone all the time. She cuddles the babies and likes to read them stories and sing them lullabies. She also plays with her dolls, making them tiny blankets and houses with leaves and twigs.

These friendly little gnome sisters will have lots of fun adventures in your home. Their cousins Aspen and Hunter (as shown together on page 32) can be made following the same instructions, with some overalls and a new hairdo.

FINISHED HEIGHT: 14" (35.5cm), without hat

SUPPLIES

Templates (pages 112–113) • Fabric for 1 doll: 3 coordinating fat quarters for the main body, hat, and apron or overalls; 1 skin-tone fat quarter; sherpa suede for boots (1 fat quarter per pair) • Stuffing • Yarn for hair and optional scarf • 4mm bicone crystals or embroidery floss for eyes • Crochet hook suitable for yarn size chosen (if making scarf) • Thread • Basic sewing tools (pages 8–10)

FABRICS SHOWN: from the Sorbet and It's a Boy Thing collections, courtesy Michael Miller Fabrics

INSTRUCTIONS

Cut out all gnome doll pattern pieces, using the templates provided. The gnome dolls are constructed in two major sections: the front side and the back side.

FRONT SIDE OF DOLL

1. To make the front of the gnome doll, gather 1 head piece, 1 chest, 2 arms, 2 hands, front lower body/leg piece and (optional) apron.

2. Place the head piece right side down on top of the chest piece (which is right side up). Stitch these pieces together on the flat edge of the head and the top edge of the chest.

3. Open and lay the sewn pieces flat, right side up.

NOTE: Skip steps 4–9 if you are not adding the apron.

4. To make the apron, fold a double hem on both short sides of the apron, approximately ⅛" (3mm) each time, and sew the tiny hemmed edges with a top stitch.

5. Fold the bottom edge in the same manner as step 4 and top stitch the tiny double hem.

6. Run a stitch of thread (contrasting if desired) across the top raw edge of the apron, for gathering the fabric evenly once pinned.

7. Place the apron right side down on top of the chest piece, lining up the raw edge of the apron to the bottom raw edge of the chest piece, leaving ¼" (6mm) on each side of the chest piece for sewing the body together later. Pin each side.

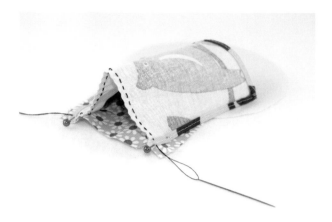

8. Pin the center of the apron to the center of the chest piece.

9. Tighten the gathering stitch, and pin the apron in between the first 3 pins. Do not remove the gathered thread yet.

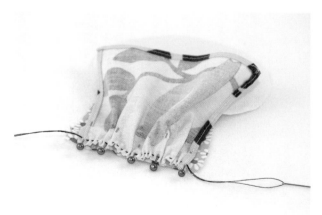

10. Lay the front lower body/leg piece on top of the apron, right side down, so the raw top edge of the lower body/leg piece is aligned with the bottom edge of the chest piece/apron. Re-pin to connect all three pieces.

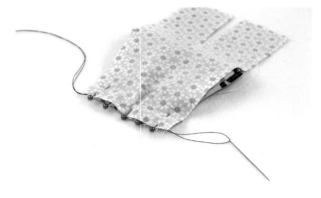

11. Sew straight across this edge and remove the pins and gathered thread.

12. Open the pieces to lie flat, right side up.

13. Place one arm piece right side down on top of the chest piece. Center the end of the arm to the side of the chest piece, so there is room for seam allowance on both the neck and armpit. Pin.

14. Pin the other arm on the other side of the chest piece and sew both arms in place.

15. Now sew the hands onto the ends of the arms. Place the hands right side down, with the thumbs up, then pin and sew each hand on. Set the doll front aside.

BACK SIDE OF DOLL

1. To sew the back of the doll, you'll need the remaining head piece, upper back, 2 arms, 2 hands and the 2 back lower body/leg pieces.

2. Take the two lower body/leg pieces, line them up and place them right sides together.

3. Sew only 1" (2.5cm) of the center seam at the top. Then sew only 1" (2.5cm) of the center seam at the bottom of the back (not the bottom of the legs). The open length in between will stay open for turning and stuffing.

4. You should have already cut the triangle (dart) from the outer edge of the legs; if not, do this now. Use the template to be sure you cut the dart in the correct position.

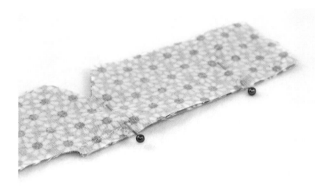

5. Lay the head piece right side down on top of the upper back piece (which is right side up). Sew these pieces together on the flat edge of the head and the top edge of the upper back as shown in step 2 of the doll front.

6. Open and lay the sewn pieces flat, right side up.

7. Lay the back leg piece right side down, so the raw top edge of the back leg piece is aligned with the bottom edge of the upper back piece. Sew.

8. Repeat steps 12–15 of the doll front to sew the back sides of the arms and hands to the upper back and leg pieces of the doll.

9. Fold each leg dart one at a time so that the outer edge is aligned and right sides are facing each other. Sew the dart together. Repeat on the other side. The front leg piece will now be the same length as the back leg piece.

ASSEMBLING THE DOLL

1. Place two ear pieces right sides together, and sew from one corner up to the point, and back down the other side to the opposite corner. Make sure to use a lock stitch at the start and end. Leave the flat edge open to allow for turning right side out. Clip the edges. Turn the ear right side out using a turning tool. Repeat this step for the other ear.

2. Pin the ears in place, using the guides on the templates.

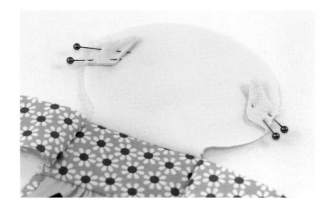

3. Take the back piece of the doll and lay it right side down on top of the front piece.

4. Pin the body together, lining up the seams, ends and armpits.

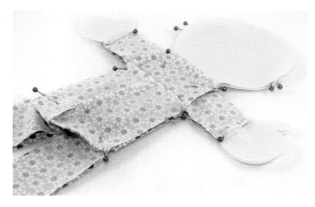

5. Sew from one ankle on the outer edge up the outside of the leg, all the way around the arm and hand and up the neck, sewing only a small portion of the head (approximately 1" [2.5cm]). Be careful not to sew the apron into the seam during this step.

6. Repeat step 5 on the other side of the body.

7. Sew the inseam, from the inside of one ankle up the leg, around the center and down the other inside leg to the opposite ankle.

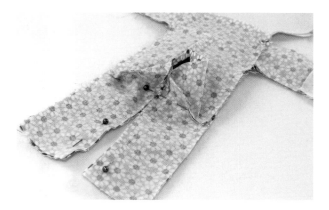

8. Sew each foot by taking 2 pieces, right sides facing, and stitching them together. Leave the flat edge open for turning, making sure to use a lock stitch at the start and end. Clip and notch the edges and use a turning tool to turn right side out.

9. To attach the feet to the doll's ankles, lay the doll body face up. Insert the feet into the leg holes toes first, with the toes pointing upward. The seams on the foot will line up to the centers of the ankle, just as the center of the foot will line up with the seams on the ankle. The feet are sewn on last in this manner so the feet will face forward and not off to the side.

10. Pin the seams and center marks in place and carefully hand sew (or machine sew, if you'd prefer) all the way around each ankle.

Tip If you want the feet to face off to the sides, sew the feet to the ankles after step 2 of assembling the doll, before pinning and sewing the doll's front and back sides together.

FOR LONG HAIR

1. To prep the yarn hair, determine the desired length for your doll and add 2" (5.1cm). (You will have to trim the hair later, and this will prevent it from being too short.) You can easily wrap the yarn around a smooth straight-edge or board. Cut along the top and bottom edges so all of your pieces are approximately the same length and are lying side by side in a single layer.

2. Lay the doll so the back side of the doll is on top. Peel the back head piece down to expose the face or the front part of the head (with the ears pinned to it).

3. Begin laying the hair on the front part of the face, staying above the ears and placing each strand however you want it to look once finished. (The first layer will be the hair that will lie around the front of the face; the second layer lies on the back of the head.) Lay the strands side by side, with the ends up against the raw edge of the fabric. The length of the strands will lie on the face for now.

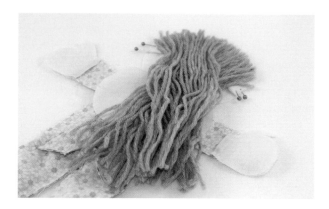

4. Once you have the strands placed that will lie around the front of the doll, position on top of that a second layer of hair that will lie on the back of the head. The back hair strands should cover the ear and also go just below the ear.

5. Lay the strands so each group is overlapping rather than trying to curve them downward, so they stay in place better. If you want it fuller, position a third layer.

Tip Keep in mind that all the hair has to stay on top of the fabric and be sewn inward. Eventually, it will have to be pulled through the neck and out the back when turning inside out. If you layer too much or the yarn is very thick, it won't fit through the neck opening.

6. When all the hair is in place, hold down the ends of the hair on the top of the head as best you can so they do not move.

7. Gently and carefully twist the long hair strands with your other hand, while keeping pressure on the top ends.

8. Once you have twisted all of the yarn to the end of the "ponytail," tuck the ponytail into the neck cavity.

9. Once it's all tucked inside, carefully lift your hand off the head and cover the hair with the back of the head piece, without letting the strand ends move.

10. Carefully pin all the way around the head. All the hair should now be in a pinned head pocket, with only a small portion of the strands sticking out.

Tip If you have a hard time pulling the hair strands out, use a crochet hook to help work them out gently. It will be tight so take your time.

11. Sew from one side of the neck all the way around the top of the head to the other side of the neck. Be careful not to sew the tip of the ears into the seam during this step.

12. Stitch all the way around the head once more for extra strength to prevent any hair being pulled out while it's being turned right side out (and while being played with).

13. Clip and notch in and around all the curves, making sure to clip the tight curves in between the thumbs and fingers, in the armpits and between the legs, being careful not to cut the seams or get too close to them.

14. Before turning the hair and head right side out, check the armpits and the neck seams and make sure all pieces are sewn in thoroughly, and that the apron was not sewn into the side seams.

15. Begin to turn the doll right side out through the opening in the back, starting with the hair.

16. Carefully pull the ends of the hair through the neck and out of the back. Continue until all of the hair ends are pulled through.

17. Prior to stuffing, double-check the ears and hair to be sure they were all sewn into the seams properly, and that the ear tips were not sewn into the head seam accidentally.

18. Pull the rest of the hair out and then the head and upper body.

19. Using a turning tool, turn the thumb right side out and then the hands and feet.

20. Gently stuff the doll's feet, legs, thumbs, hands and arms to the desired firmness. Stuff the head and then the body last. Once the doll is sufficiently stuffed, close the back with a ladder stitch (see page 14).

21. Straighten out all the hair strands prior to trimming. A little at a time is best, because you can always trim off more but you can't add it back once cut. The back hairs are going to be shorter than the sides, so trim the sides first, then the back as necessary. You can also cut bangs if you'd like, straight across or at an angle, as Piper has.

FOR SHORT HAIR

1. Prep the shorter yarn hair the same way you would the longer hair, referring to long hair step 1. Cut it into smaller segments approximately 3" (7.6cm) long.

2. Lay the doll so the front side is on top (unlike in the long-hair instructions). Peel the front head piece down to expose the back of the head.

3. Take a section of yarn and lay the strands in the center of the back of the head. Stitch the hair straight down the center of the fabric.

4. Fold all of the hair over to one side and position another segment of hair and stitch it down on a slight diagonal. This should be approximately ½" to ¾" (1.3cm to 1.9cm) away from the center.

5. Fold the hair from the second stitching over to the other side again and position a third segment of hair and stitch it down. This again should be ½" to ¾" (1.3cm to 1.9cm) away from the second stitch line.

6. One you've done the third segment, flip all of the hair to expose the bald half and place two segments of hair on this side to match.

7. The inside of the back of the head should look like the lines are fanned out toward the top and tapered in toward the bottom.

8. Flip the doll so the back is on top and peel the head back to expose the face. Add a single layer of hair to the front of the doll's face from just below the ear all the way around the top of the head to underneath the other ear.

9. Close the head the same way as described in the long hair steps 9–10, making sure you guide all the short hair ends toward the center of the head or into the neck cavity. The more hair you add, the harder it will be to turn right side out (and the hat will become snug as well).

10. Finish the doll following the same process described in the long hair steps 11–21. Trim the short hair accordingly.

EYES

Follow the directions on page 16 for adding bead eyes to your doll. If this is for a small child, use embroidery floss for the eyes instead (page 17) to prevent choking hazards.

REVERSIBLE BOOTS

Make 2 per doll.

1. To sew the boots, do not cut the fabric first. If you purchased the first cut of the bolt, the edge is already going to be sewn for your top edge of the boots. If not, you will need to prep the top edge first. (To prep top edge: Cut 1 long strip of the fur, approximately 6" × 24" (15.2cm × 61cm). With the fur face down and the smooth side up, fold a single hem along the top edge ⅜" (10mm) so the fur is now along the top edge, and sew a top stitch. This stitch can be straight, decorative or hand stitched.)

2. Fold the long piece in half lengthwise, furry sides together, and pin in place. (If working with smaller pieces, pin 2 pieces furry sides together.)

3. Lay the template on top and line it up to the top of the folded edge. Trace the template onto the fabric pattern piece with a fabric marker.

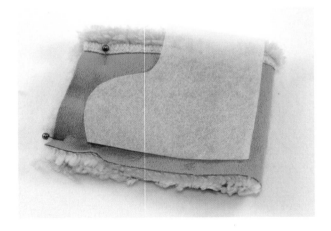

4. Sew a ¼" (6mm) straight stitch on the inside of the marked outline.

5. Cut the boot shape out ¼" (6mm) away from the seam on the marked outline, being careful not to cut the seams.

6. Vigorously rub and fluff the edge of the boot (over a garbage can) to soften the edge and to remove any loosened sherpa fibers. The boots can be worn suede-side out (as shown) or fuzzy-side out, which will hide the seam.

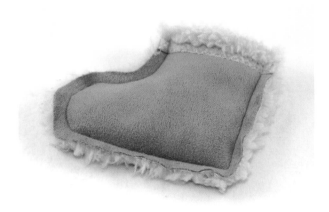

REVERSIBLE HAT

1. Place the 2 hat pieces right sides together and sew the long curved edge from one side to the other, and notch the curved seam.

2. Open the two pieces and pin the sewn ends together.

3. Sew one side of the hat 1" (2.5cm) above the pinned seams, over the seam and down to the tip of the other side.

4. Fold the hat in half, so the tips of each hat line up. Sew from the tip to approximately 1½" (3.8cm) down. This will keep the tips of the hat together when turning the hat right side out after completion.

5. There will be a small opening on one side of the hat (in the pictures, it is the red flower side that has been left open). Gently turn the hat right side out through this opening.

6. Once the hat is turned right side out, you will notice a bulky area from the seams. Poke this section out, then flatten your seams and fold them to take away the bulk.

7. The opening on the side of the hat can now be stitched closed with a ladder stitch. Be careful not to thread the needle through to the reverse side of the hat.

REVERSIBLE OVERALLS

1. To make the straps for the overalls, take the two thin Fabric B pieces and follow the binding steps on page 13.

2. Pin one end of the straps to the top edge of the Fabric A bib piece on the narrower edge, pointing them down toward the wider edge. The straps should be placed ½" (1.3cm) away from the side edges.

3. Place the reverse side of the bib piece (Fabric B) on top, right sides together, and re-pin to prevent the straps from moving.

4. Sew from one bottom corner up the side, over the top and down the other side to the opposite corner.

5. Trim the top corners at an angle, turn the bib right side out and top stitch the sewn edge.

6. Take all four overall bottom pieces and sew 2 matching pieces together at a time, only on the curved center edges.

7. Open up one set of the shorts right side up (Fabric A), place the finished bib piece matching side down, and pin the center of the bib to the center seam of the shorts. The raw edges should be together.

8. Place a short set made of the contrast (Fabric B) fabric facedown on top of that and pin in place. Sew across the top raw edge, leaving ½" (1.3cm) at each end unstitched and sewing the bib in between.

9. Flip the contrast (Fabric B) side open and the bib as well. Place the matching back side of the (Fabric A) shorts right side down on top (of Fabric A) and sew the outer edges all the way from the top to the bottom.

10. On the other side of the shorts, place the contrasting (Fabric B) set right side down on top and sew the outer edges all the way from the top to the bottom.

11. Pin the inseams together for each fabric. Be sure to line up the center seams and the corners while pinning.

12. Sew the inseam edges only ½" (1.3cm), leaving the inside of the legs open.

13. Fold the shorts in half and line up the center of the inseams and pin all 4 layers together.

14. Sew the inseams from the ½" (1.3cm) mark to the other ½" (1.3cm) mark. Do not sew the corners together. Remove all pins.

15. Flip the shorts through to the overalls side, to find the waistline that has not been sewn yet.

16. Turn the overalls right side out through this opening.

17. Fold the outer fabric inward, and the contrast fabric inward at the waistline so right sides are facing, and conceal the raw edges. Pin in place.

18. Pin the strap ends into the back waistline of the shorts, approximately ¾" to 1" (1.9cm to 2.5cm) away from the center seam, and between the 2 layers of fabric.

19. Top stitch all the way around the waist, including the front just under the bib. Be careful to move the straps out of the way during this step.

20. Finish the hems of the leg openings by folding the outer and contrast fabrics in the same manner as in step 17, then pin and finish with a top stitch.

SCARF (OPTIONAL)

You can crochet a simple scarf for your gnome by working a chain stitch to the desired length, using a crochet hook and the yarn of your choice.

CHAIN STITCH

After placing the hook through a slip knot, wrap the yarn around the hook. Draw the yarn through the loop on the hook (1 chain made). Repeat this step to the desired length. Then cut the yarn and feed the end through the last chain. Pull tight and trim the end.

Adventurer's Backpack

It's Nature Thursday in the pine grove and all the gnomes are ready for a fun day of trekking. Stick close to these gnomes and they'll show you the way. Aspen is an adventurer and loves exploring the world around him. He scales tall cliffs and trees, and seeks the things he needs to make ziplines, swings and rope ladders. He loves bugs and takes special care of the ones that help grow flowers and crops. He also keeps a journal in his backpack to write all about his travels.

His younger brother Hunter likes to tell jokes and silly stories to anyone listening. Sometimes he sneaks into the freshly picked bucket of hobblebush berries and eats them all before anyone catches him. Other times, he will stuff as many into his backpack as he can to save for later.

Good things come in small packages. Make a backpack for each gnome or for other favorite dolls or stuffed animals. It can also work well for holding gift cards or small gifts. You can make the backpack even easier by eliminating the inside and outside pockets, or by using elastic on the top rim instead of the grommets and pull straps.

FINISHED SIZE: 6" × 5½" (15.2cm × 14cm)

SUPPLIES

Templates (page 114) • Fabric: 1 fat quarter or ¼ yard (.3m) for outer layer • 1 fat quarter for lining • 4½" (11.4cm) strip of ¼" (6mm) non-rolling elastic • (8) ⅛" (3mm) eyelet sets • Button (fabric-covered if desired) • Awl or eyelet pliers • Binding maker tool or bias tape maker (optional) • Thread • Basic sewing tools (pages 8–10)

FABRICS SHOWN: from the It's a Boy Thing collection, courtesy Michael Miller Fabrics; 21-wale corduroy by Robert Kaufman Fabrics

INSTRUCTIONS

1. Cut out all backpack pattern pieces, using the templates provided or by cutting with a straightedge and cutting mat. (If you would like to cut longer pieces for the straps and sew it all at once, you can easily add the lengths together and cut them down later.)

> *Tip* Old corduroy pants or denim jeans can be recycled to form a durable outer layer for this backpack.

2. Take the 2 pieces for the pull straps and the 1 button loop piece and follow the instructions on page 13 to make your own binding, or use one of your binding-making tools, following the manufacturer's instructions.

3. When all the binding folds are pressed, top stitch the 2 folded edges together, along the entire length of each piece and set aside.

4. To make the backpack straps and the backpack hook loop, take a strip of the fabric lining and a strip of the outer fabric and place them right sides together.

5. Sew the lengthwise edge on both sides.

6. Turn right side out, pressing if necessary.

7. Top stitch the lengthwise edge on both sides.

8. Repeat steps 4–7 to sew the other strap and the loop, and set them all aside.

9. Prepare the 2 outer pockets by folding a ⅜" (10mm) double hem (see page 12) on the top edge.

10. Top stitch the lower folded edge so you have room for the elastic.

11. Thread the elastic through and secure it ⅛" (3mm) away from the raw edge of the pocket with a little stitch on both ends. Doing this now will make sewing it into the side seams easier later on. If you have precut the elastic pieces to 2¼" (5.6cm), use fabric tweezers to pull the other end out, or keep it long and mark 2¼" (5.6cm), then trim after sewing.

12. Fold the corners and sew a ½" (1.3cm) dart on the 2 bottom corners of each outer pocket.

13. Trim the tiny excess corners off, turn right side out and set aside.

14. Using an ⅛" (3mm) seam allowance, fold a double hem on the top long edge of the inside pocket.

15. Press the folds as you go along. Pin if necessary and sew a top stitch along the top edge of the inside pocket.

16. Fold and press the sides of the inside pocket the same way, but do not sew a top stitch just yet.

17. Place the back piece of the lining right side up. Place the pocket piece right side down and centered, with the bottom edge of the pocket 2" (5.1cm) from the bottom edge of the lining. Pin in place and sew this raw edge from one side to the other.

18. Flip the inside pocket right side up toward the top edge, and top stitch both sides and the bottom in place.

19. Sew the bottom panel of the lining to the bottom edge of the back lining panel, with right sides together. Use an inset seam by leaving ¼" (6mm) unstitched on each end. Lock in your stitches.

20. Open these two pieces and lay the front piece of the lining on the opposite side of the bottom, right sides together, and sew this edge with an inset seam also.

21. Before placing the side panel, fold the front and back panels so they are diagonal, and reveal one entire side edge.

22. Place a side panel right side down and sew this bottom side edge together, being careful not to catch in the front and back. This sewn seam does not need to be inset as do the front and back edges.

23. Repeat steps 21–22 for the other side panel of the lining.

34

24. Open all pieces and begin to sew the four side seams together, from the top to the bottom, and set aside. NOTE: When you sew the side seams from the top to the bottom of the backpack, your top edge is guaranteed to line up properly.

25. Fold the lining flap piece in half to find the center mark. Place the button loop on that mark and pin in place. (Prior to pinning and sewing, adjust the length of this loop according to size of your button.)

26. Place the outer flap piece right side down, on top, sew the curved edge, then notch the edge.

27. Turn the flap right side out and top stitch the curved edge.

28. Place the outer back side panel right side down. Using a straightedge to assist you, place both raw edges of the hook strap, side by side. The two straps should meet in the center, up at the top edge and be pinned in place.

29. Place the top of the straps, one on each side, directly beside the hook piece and pin in place.

30. Pin the bottom of the straps approximately ¾" (1.9cm) away from the side edges. This will make them slightly diagonal; however, you can place them straight if you prefer.

31. Sew the bottom outer panel to the bottom edge of the back outer panel, using an inset seam (as shown in step 19).

32. Open these 2 pieces and lay the front panel of the outer backpack on the other side of the bottom panel, right sides together, and sew this edge with an inset seam also.

33. As you did in step 21, fold the front and back panels so they are diagonal and reveal a side edge.

34. Place and pin the pocket to the bottom of the outer backpack side panel. The 2 dart seams should line up with the corners of the side edge.

35. Place the side panel with pocket right side down on top and sew these bottom raw edges together. This sewn seam does not need to be inset as the front and back edges do.

36. Repeat steps 33–35 for the other pocket and side panel of the outer fabric.

37. Open all pieces and pin the pull straps ½" (1.3cm) down from the top of the back panel.

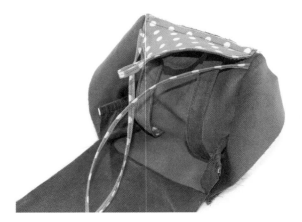

38. Sew the 4 side seams together, from the top to the bottom.

39. To prevent the lining from pulling away from the outer fabric, sew the 2 long edges of the bottoms to each other.

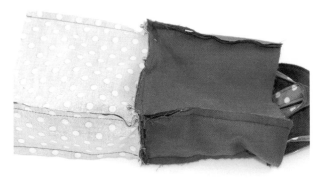

40. Turn the outer fabric of the bag right side out so the lining is now on the inside.

Tip If you want to eliminate the small metal eyelets, you can opt for buttonholes instead and skip steps 45 and 46 coming up. If you prefer to lose the holes altogether, you can skip steps 44–47 and place elastic between the two layers, from one rear side seam and around the front to the other rear side seam (not the back).

41. Line up the 4 corner seams and turn both the outer fabric and the lining fabric in ¼" (6mm) and pin together.

42. Place your button centered on the front of the back-pack according to the size and loop length and sew into place. Be sure not to sew the button to the lining.

43. Finish pinning the top of the lining to the outer fabric and topstitch it into place. Do not sew the straps as you complete this step.

44. Using a fabric marker, mark 4 equally spaced spots on the front panel and 2 spots on each side panel for the eyelets. The holes should be about ⅜" (10mm) from the folded edge, to line up with the straps.

45. Using an awl or eyelet pliers, punch holes just large enough for the pull straps on these 8 marks.

Tip Before punching holes in your back-pack, test your tool on fabric scraps. If the fabric is too thin, it may chew up your fabric. If this happens, use a scrap of natural batting to thicken the backpack edge while punching the holes.

46. Follow the manufacturer's instructions to fasten eyelets into the holes.

47. Weave the pull straps in and out through the eyelets or buttonholes until they are both coming out of the front center eyelets or buttonholes.

48. Tie the very ends of the straps into a knot to prevent any unraveling.

Mouse Pals: SHERBET & PISTACHIO

When the gnomes are away, the mice will play! This is Sherbet and Pistachio. Right now they are supposed to be helping the gnomes gather firewood and berries, but they couldn't pass up a chance to play awhile before getting to work. These lifelong friends love to swing, play hopscotch and jump rope when the sun is rising and setting.

All of the mice around here are very important for the gnomes. They help dig holes in the ground so that the gnomes have a safe and cool place to put their hobblebush berries during the summer months. In the winter, they help pull the gnome sleds across the snow-covered valley to search for more firewood. They are happy little creatures and love to cuddle with their gnome family at day's end.

This little mouse is sure to be a child's best friend. On the first day of school, at the doctor's office or anywhere you want to bring a little cuddle with you, this mouse will be happy to go along. This cute project is a perfect way to use up some of your fun fabric scraps that are too small for other bigger endeavors.

FINISHED HEIGHT: 6" (15.2cm)

SUPPLIES

Templates (page 114) • Fabric: 1 fat eighth (per mouse) • Stuffing • Pipe cleaner (or chenille stem) for tail (optional) • Embroidery floss or 2 round beads for eyes (optional) • Thread • Basic sewing tools (pages 8–10)

FABRICS SHOWN: from the Daisy Chain and Belle collections by Amy Butler

INSTRUCTIONS

1. Cut out all mouse pattern pieces. Sew all of the ears, arms, legs and the tail by placing 2 like pieces right sides together, sewing from one end around to the other end, and leaving the flat edges open for turning. Be sure to lock in your stitches.

2. Clip and notch all of the edges and curves, making sure to clip the inside curve on the front ankle of the feet. Be careful not to clip the seams.

3. Using a turning tool, turn all of these pieces right side out.

4. Stuff the arms and legs to the desired fullness, but do not overstuff.

> *Tip* You can leave the tail as-is to be floppy, or if you want to stuff the tail, use stuffing or a pipe cleaner (or chenille stem) to make the tail bendable. Let about ¾" (1.9cm) of the pipe cleaner extend out from the end of the tail and curl it in a spiral to keep it from being pulled out from the seam.

5. Lay the head pieces right side up.

6. Place an ear in each dart on the head so that the raw edge of the ear is in between the slit, and the tip of the ear is pointing toward the nose. There should be approximately ¼" (6mm) of space left above the ear so the top of the head can be sewn together.

7. Sew the ear into the dart at a slight angle, starting at ¼" (6mm) up at the top and narrowing to a point just past the base of the ears.

8. Place a body piece right side up.

9. Place an arm on top of the body piece and align the raw edges. The arm should be in the center of the top edge of the body piece with the seams to the sides.

10. Take a finished head piece and lay it face down, centered, on top of the arm and body. Align the raw edges, and sew across this edge.

11. Lay the 2 body pieces right sides together. Pin the edges at the ears and on both sides of the neck.

12. Pin the tail on the back side of the mouse ½" (1.3cm) up from the bottom edge, so that the tail is on the inside.

13. Sew all the way around the mouse from the bottom corner, up around the head (do not sew the ears into the seam) and back down to the other corner. Leave the bottom flat edge open. Turn the mouse right side out.

14. Attach the legs by first pinning them to the front of the mouse, one on each side of the center body seam, and then sewing them. The toes should be facing toward the chest during this step.

15. Stuff the nose, head and then the body.

16. Unfold the legs and close the back bottom of the mouse using a ladder stitch. It may be easiest to sew the back of the mouse body to the back of the legs first, then sew the remaining edges closed.

17. Follow the instructions on page 17 to add some embroidery eyes to your mouse (or page 16 for bead eyes, if desired).

Magical Mushrooms

On this very special day in the pine grove, excitement can be felt everywhere. All of the gnomes and their furry friends are gathering for one of their annual celebrations, encircled by the oldest mushrooms. As the special mushroom circle grows each year, they find more reasons to gather inside the ring. Today, they celebrate autumn's arrival and give thanks for the many things they have. They each share what they are grateful for, followed by a bountiful harvest feast. The fun, games and laughter last all night.

In just a few months a peaceful hush will fill the valley as the sun sets earlier each day, and snowflakes begin to fall. On the shortest day of the year, the gnomes all gather in the mushroom ring once again, to call the sun back to warm them and help return the valley to a luscious green.

With this being the easiest pattern in the book, make one or many, in various sizes and with new or recycled fabrics for variety (another great stash-buster project). Make your own mushroom ring for dancing, singing and celebrating in.

FINISHED SIZES (height): 4" (10.2cm), 8½" (21.6cm), 9" (22.9cm)

SUPPLIES

Templates (page 115) • Fabric: 1–2 fat quarters for size small, 2 fat quarters for size large • Stuffing • Thread • Basic sewing tools (pages 8–10)

FABRICS SHOWN: from the Dandy Damask, It's a Boy Thing and Mini Mikes collections, courtesy Michael Miller Fabrics

INSTRUCTIONS

1. Cut out all the mushroom pattern pieces, including the center gray circle of the mushroom cap base. (Cut out the center by folding the base in half twice and then cutting the folded tip, as shown in step 6 on page 65.) Place 2 of the mushroom cap pieces right sides together and sew from the bottom up to the top, leaving ¼" (6mm) unstitched at the tip. Lock in your stitches.

2. Open them right side up and lay another top piece right side down, and then sew from the bottom edge to the top, leaving ¼" (6mm) unstitched. Now there are 3 pieces attached.

3. Sew the last top piece to the other 3 in the same manner, and then connect the first piece to the last piece.

4. Fold the stem piece in half, right sides together, and stitch ½" (1.3cm) of the straight edge from the top and ½" (1.3cm) from the bottom, leaving the center of the straight edge open for turning. Lock in your stitches.

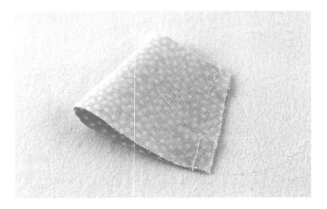

5. Fold the mushroom base in quarters and press to crease. Then fold the bottom edge of the stem and crease to evenly line up the pieces to pin in place.

6. While the stem is still inside out, pin the bottom of the stem to the mushroom base (wrong side facing outward) at the 4 crease marks first.

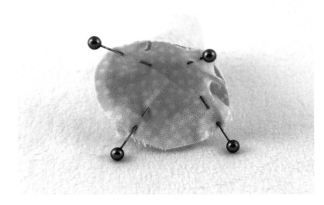

7. Line up the spaces in between each pin, and place pins to hold them together. This step is more important for larger mushrooms.

8. Sew the pieces together around the edge. (Hand sewing this step may be easier for the smaller mushrooms.)

9. Turn the sewn stem right side out.

10. Place the inside ring of the mushroom cap base (which is the underside of the mushroom head) onto the top of the stem, so that the right side is facing down.

11. Pin the underside ring in place and sew it by hand all the way around.

12. Open the mushroom cap and place the stem inside, with right sides on the inside.

13. Pin in place if necessary at each seam, and sew all the way around the edge of the mushroom cap.

14. Carefully notch the side edges and rim of the mushroom cap and base of the stem.

15. Turn the entire mushroom inside out and stuff to the desired fullness.

16. Use a ladder stitch to close the stem opening.

Tip For smaller mushrooms, it is easier to make the caps and stems, stuff each one, and then sew the stem to the center of the cap base with a ladder stitch.

2

Coastal Waters

The majority of my life has been spent along the East Coast, listening to waves break on the shore with sand between my toes and salt in the air. My everyday experiences inspired these seaside projects, which I hope will in turn inspire you.

Morton the Painted Turtle

For those of you who don't know me, I am Morton, a painted turtle. I was born on Rocky Pond and over the past few years have traveled far and wide, ending up on the sandy beaches of Maine.

I wake early in the morning underwater and eat tiny fish and sea grass. After breakfast, I lie on the warm sand or rocks, and sometimes on floating driftwood to catch some sun. I need lots of sunshine to keep my shell strong, so I will happily do this all day. I walk very slowly and will eat occasionally along the way. Sometimes I play hide-and-seek, pulling my head, feet and tail into my shell to hide from big birds and raccoons. My sturdy shell protects me, but it's also fun to play hide-and-seek.

You can make a few shells for this turtle and switch them up once in a while. A turtle always loves a new shell. Who wouldn't?

FINISHED LENGTH: 15" (38.1cm)

SUPPLIES

Templates (page 116) • Fabric for turtle shell (includes rim): 3 fat quarters in various patterns, or ⅔ yard (.6m) total • Fabric for turtle body: 2 fat quarters (different patterns), or ½ yard (.5m) total • Batting (optional; slightly less than a fat quarter's worth) • Stuffing • Embroidery floss • Thread • Basic sewing tools (pages 8–10)

FABRICS SHOWN: from Midwest Modern collection by Amy Butler

TURTLE SHELL

1. Cut out all of the turtle pattern pieces for the shell and the body. Also cut a 3½" x 41" (8.9cm x 104.1cm) fabric strip for the shell rim (if using a fat quarter, connect two shorter strips together).

Tip Although this belly piece is going to be double-sided, only one side will be visible. You can use a solid print for the shell's underbelly that will not be seen, if you'd prefer.

2. Fold and press the turtle belly piece to mark the center of the top, bottom and sides. Sew the belly pieces right sides together, being careful to only sew the neck, arm, leg and tail openings. Clip the curves.

3. Turn the belly right side out, and top stitch all the same edges you stitched in step 2.

4. Fold and press the turtle underbelly piece to mark the center of the top, bottom and sides. Place special pins at these center marks to use as references.

5. Layer the following pieces right side up: the underbelly piece and then, centered on top, the belly piece you just made. Be sure that the belly side you want visible when the turtle is complete is showing now.

6. Place the shell rim strip up at the front center of the turtle, right side down. Place it so there is a ½" (1.3cm) seam allowance to the left of the front center mark.

7. Pin the edge of the shell rim all the way around until the ends overlap.

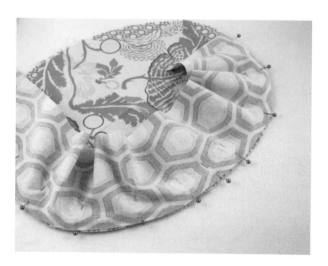

8. Sew these ends right sides together and trim if necessary. Press the ends open.

9. Using a ¼" (6mm) seam allowance, only sew the 2 long sides approximately 2" (5.1cm) above and 2" (5.1cm) below the side centers. This step will help later when closing the shell after stuffing.

10. Fold the rim in half lengthwise starting at the front center seam, and now pull over and pin the opposite raw edge to the pinned outside edge (this will be stuffed later, and should show as right sides facing out). Be sure the pin heads face out.

11. Fold the outer shell piece in quarters and press first to mark your center points as in step 4.

12. Place the outer shell piece right side down on top of the other pinned shell pieces. The shell rim should be laying toward the inside with raw edges pinned.

13. Line up the center creases of the outer shell piece to the other pieces and pin these four points in place. This piece is much bigger than the other pieces to give the shell room for plenty of stuffing.

14. About 1" (2.5cm) from the front and back center pins, to the left and right of each pin, tuck ⅜" (10mm) of the fabric underneath to create a knife pleat, and pin.

15. In the same manner as step 14, create knife pleats on the sides. These pleats will take up all the extra slack on this outer shell piece.

16. Pin the remaining raw edges together as needed.

17. With a ⅜" (10mm) seam allowance, sew the back half of the body from one side at the pleat, down and around past the other pleat.

Tip Be sure to sew the pleats in steps 17–18, as it will be difficult to gather and sew them after the shell is stuffed.

18. Repeat step 17 on the front half. Once sewn, both sides of the turtle shell should have a 3" (7.6cm) opening for turning and later for stuffing.

19. Find the opening between the rim and the outer shell and gently turn the entire piece right side out.

20. Through one side, carefully stuff only half of the rim up toward the front center, and then toward the back center to prevent tearing at the seam.

21. Through the other side, carefully stuff the other half of the rim, up to the center and down to the back. Be sure not to overstuff.

22. When the rim is sufficiently stuffed, pin the raw edges in place and hand-stitch or machine stitch the rim closed from the inside on both sides of the shell. This will help to prevent the rim from shifting while sewing it fully closed.

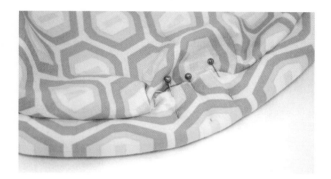

23. Carefully stuff the shell from both sides.

24. Using a ladder stitch, fold down the seam allowance of the shell and sew the rim closed.

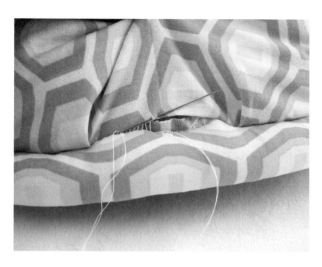

25. Gently place the rim under your sewing machine foot (you may have to remove your foot to get it underneath), and sew a top stitch all the way around the inside edge. This will cause your underneath side to be sewn blind, but will add some protection to the edges when placing the body through the small arm and leg holes. Set the finished shell aside.

Tip Be careful not to pull and stretch the openings on the sides. Do not overstuff, as this will make it difficult to put the turtle body inside the underbelly.

TURTLE BODY

1. Begin by sewing the 2 head pattern pieces together, with right sides facing. Leave the neck open for turning and stuffing. Lock in your stitches at the beginning and end of each piece.

2. Sew the arms, legs and tail in the same manner.

3. Clip and notch the edges of each of these 6 pieces, making sure not to cut the seams.

4. Turn these pieces right side out and stuff accordingly, without overstuffing. Leave room at the ends for attaching to the body.

5. Fold and press both turtle body pieces to mark the centers of the front, back and sides.

6. Place one piece of the turtle body face up. Place the turtle belly pattern piece on top for reference.

7. In the center of each "opening," place the arms and legs so the raw edges meet. Seams should be at the sides. The arms and legs should be lying toward the inside on top of the turtle belly piece (arms curving upward and legs curving downward). Pin all into place.

8. Before you pin the head and tail into place, you will need to flatten the openings, so seams are lined up together.

9. Line up the head seams with the center front of the turtle body piece and pin in place. The head should be laying toward the center of the turtle body piece, with raw edges lined up and chin pointing upward.

10. Line up the tail seams with the center back of the turtle body piece and pin in place. Again, the tail should be lying toward the center of the turtle body piece.

11. Remove the turtle belly pattern piece that was used as a reference guide before moving on.

12. Place the other turtle body piece on top, right side down.

13. Starting at the front, line up the center fold with the head seam and pin the top piece to cover the head.

14. Line up the center crease on the back with the tail seam, and pin this piece to cover the tail.

15. Line up the side folds and pin the two turtle body pieces together.

16. Pin the remaining perimeter of the turtle body. All of the extremities should be on the inside of what now looks like a pouch.

17. On one side of the turtle body, begin sewing approximately 1" (2.5cm) down from the center fold, all the way around the body. Leave a 2" (5.1cm) opening to turn the body right side out. Lock in your stitches at the beginning and the end.

18. Carefully pull the arms and legs out one by one, then the head and tail. Be sure to check that all the raw edges have been sewn into the seam edge properly. If any slipped, fix them before moving on. This is very common if they are well stuffed; it's a very tight fit.

19. Top stitch all the way around the edge of the body to secure the head, tail and extremities. Leave the 2" (5.1cm) opening for stuffing.

20. Stuff the body very lightly with fluff, or cut a piece of batting slightly smaller than the turtle body pattern piece to place inside. If you overstuff, you will not be able to get the body into the underbelly. Top stitch the side of the body closed.

21. Stitch any decorative shape you like to personalize your turtle. I have always created a freehand, elongated heart, using pins as my guides. You can use the machine or stitch by hand. Use any shape or letter; just have fun with it and make it your own.

22. To get the turtle into the underbelly, position the two back legs and tail into one front armhole. Then move the arm through the same arm hole to the other side, and finally the head. Do not pull by the arms and legs, but rather by the edge of the body, to avoid ripping. Pull the tail through and adjust the arms, legs and head as needed.

23. To remove the body from the shell, follow step 22 in reverse.

24. Add some eyes if you'd like, using a strong doll needle and embroidery floss. See page 17 for instructions.

Water Baby the Rowboat

Water Baby was born on the banks of Grace Creek in a small Maryland town. She learned her trade well, and was a hard worker back in her day. She carried many loads of crab to nearby fishermen in the hot summer sun. Sometimes the crabs nipped at her sides to get out, but she kept on going. Water Baby made a lot of great friends in the waters of Grace Creek.

As time went on, she retired from carrying the heavy crab loads each season, and now she enjoys taking children out for short rides. She loves hearing their laughter all day, and being a part of their summer adventures. Even when things are quiet in the colder months, Water Baby is a great companion for a seaside retreat.

With this reversible pattern, you will get two fun boats in one. You won't be able to stop yourself from placing little gnomes and stuffies inside this boat and rowing along through your wildest dreams and down the nearest river.

FINISHED BOAT LENGTH: 10½" (26.7cm)

SUPPLIES

Templates (page 117) • Boat fabric: 1 fat quarter for each side of the boat (Fabric A and Fabric B) • Fabric for paddles: 1 fat quarter • ¼ yard (.2m) medium-weight stabilizer • 1 fat quarter of cotton batting • Stuffing • Thread • Basic sewing tools (pages 8–10)

FABRICS SHOWN: from the Sugar & Spice collection by Amanda Herring

INSTRUCTIONS

1. Cut out the rowboat pattern pieces using the fabric of your choice, and the batting and stabilizer pieces.

2. Layer the boat side pieces in the following order, from bottom to top: batting, Fabric A (right side up), Fabric B (right side down), and the stabilizer.

3. Line all the pieces up and sew the top (longest) edge from one end to the other, using a ⅜" (10mm) seam allowance.

4. Repeat this for the other side pieces and the rear pieces of the boat; set the rear pieces aside.

5. Open up one of the boat sides and lay it right side up on the table.

6. Open the other side and lay it down, right sides together, on top of the first side. Match up like fabrics.

7. Line up the curved center seams and pin in place to prevent shifting. Sew this front curved edge from one end to the other.

8. Repeat steps 5–7 two more times, in order to attach the back of the sides to the back piece of the boat.

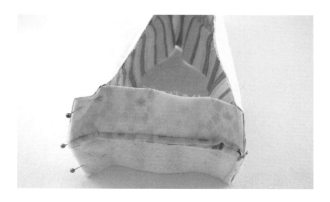

9. Clip the front curved edge of the boat's seam allowances. Do not clip the seams.

10. Open up the center seam of the front edge that you stitched first in step 7, and fold the two sides wrong sides together and pin in place. Opening the seam will reduce the bulk where the seams intersect.

11. Repeat step 10 on the back corners of the boat and pin in place.

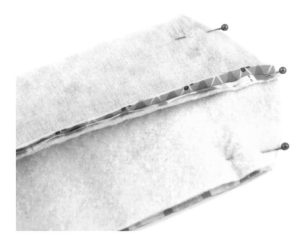

12. Once the sides of the boat are all pinned in place, top stitch around the top of the boat and along each side of each seam. It's easiest to start at the top, cross over a seam, come down along the right side of the seam, cross over the bottom raw edge of the seam, back up the left side of the seam, and cross over again to continue a top stitch along the folded edge. Continue in this box pattern around each seam to add strength.

13. Place on your table the bottom of the boat stabilizer piece and the same bottom boat fabric piece that is currently on the inside of the boat edges.

14. Place the finished boat rim (or sides) down on top. Line up the raw edges of the back section to the back edge of the boat bottom. Pin in place.

15. Place the other fabric right side down on top of these pieces, and the batting on top of that. Again, line up the edge of the bottom of the boat and pin in place.

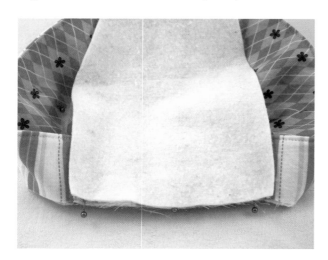

16. Sew this back/bottom edge with an inset seam, leaving a ¼" (6mm) seam allowance on each back corner. You will also need to leave a 2" (5.1cm) center opening on this edge for turning and stuffing. Lock in your stitches.

17. Pin all layers of the left and right sides of the boat to the base of the boat. The sides of the boat should be pinned toward the inside of the boat.

18. Pull the contrasting fabric and batting that is on top over the sides and pin this into place as well.

19. Sew both sides of the boat, from back to front.

> *Tip* The two back corners and the front tip of the boat will be the hardest to sew all together. If you can't sew all the corners in at once, try sewing them down without the top fabric and batting pieces. Then sew the corners afterward.

20. Through the back opening, carefully pull the boat right side out.

21. Check your back corners to be sure the raw edges are sufficiently sewn into the seam.

22. Check the front point on the bottom of the boat and be sure the side raw edges are sufficiently sewn into the seam as well. If any raw edge of the side is not sewn in (as shown below), turn the boat inside out again to fix before moving on.

23. To close up the boat, fold the raw edge inward and pin in place. With a needle and thread, sew the seam closed using a ladder stitch. Remove all pins.

PADDLES

Make 2.

1. To make each paddle, place 2 pieces of the fabric paddles together with right sides facing.

2. Place the batting piece on top of the flat paddle portion.

3. Begin sewing on the side edge, down and around the paddle, up around the handle and back down, leaving a 1" (2.5cm) opening for turning and stuffing. Clip the curves.

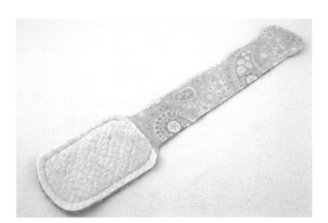

4. Using a turning tool, carefully turn the flat paddle portion right side out through the opening. Turn the handle of the paddle right side out also.

5. Top stitch the paddle. Sew another rounded corner rectangle in the center of the paddle to stiffen the paddle if you'd like.

6. Gently stuff the handle of the paddle to the desired stiffness, making sure not to overstuff.

7. Close the side of the paddle handle with a ladder stitch.

Pinchy the Lobster

I'm Pinchy, a spotted calico lobster from the coast of Maine. I have lots of family and friends, and we hang out on the dark ocean floor all day long. We try to stay far away from bright lights and lobster traps. My friends Crusher and Nova went for a walk and got caught in a trap last year, but we all got together and pulled the trap apart so they wouldn't end up on someone's dinner plate.

It seems we are pretty popular around here. I heard we are even popular as far south as Bermuda! Did you know they have pink sand there? Maine is very pretty, but I'd love to play in pink sand. Pink is my favorite color, along with baby blue. I like to collect sea glass. My collection is growing, but I have to keep it tucked away or the tides will wash it to shore.

This lobster pattern will surely take some time to cut out and piece together, but it's fun to play with and you'll want to make more. This adorable lobster is not edible, so save your butter and lemons and get sewing!

FINISHED LENGTH: 13" (33cm)

SUPPLIES

Templates (page 118) • Fabric: 2 fat quarters (or 3 for variety) • Stuffing • 2 pipe cleaners (or chenille stems) for antennae (optional) • Embroidery floss or 2 round beads for eyes (optional) • Thread • Basic sewing tools (pages 8–10)

FABRIC SHOWN: from the Out to Sea collection by Sarah Jane, courtesy Michael Miller Fabrics

TAIL AND BELLY

1. Begin preparing the knife-pleated top of the lobster tail piece by cutting out a photocopy of the lobster tail pattern as a guide and getting the largest fabric piece. These knife pleats will all go in the same direction, but folded back and forth. The flat width of the knife pleats alternates from just over 1" (2.5cm) to about ⅜" (10mm). When completed, each pleat will be ⅜" (10mm), with extra seam allowance on the top edge and on the bottom edge of the piece.

2. Lay the guide on top of the fabric, lining it up with the short edge. Mark a line across the fabric to match up with the base of the first blue mark of 1⅛" (2.9cm). Fold and press this line, with the wrong sides of the fabric touching.

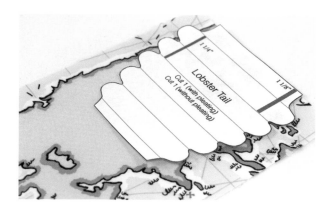

3. The next fold will be at ⅜" (10mm) with right sides touching. You can lay the guide on the fabric again and mark this line visually, and then pull that fabric up and over the guide to line it up. Pin in place.

So, when laying the guide up to the top edge of the fabric, your first pleat should line up with the 1⅛" (2.9cm) section. Underneath, it should line up with the ⅜" (10mm) section.

4. Fold the top segment of the guide under before proceeding, because the first pleat is a little smaller than the others.

5. Now mark and press a line across the fabric to match the base of the second blue mark, which is 1¼" (3.2cm). When you fold the fabric back, pull that fold over the guide as you did previously.

6. Continue to fold, press and pin each pleat, following the previous steps. When finished, you should have 5 pleats that all line up with the lobster tail guide from front to back. Trim any excess fabric if you started with a piece of fabric longer than 10¼" (26cm). Set the pleated and pinned piece aside.

7. Now prepare the lobster belly piece. Take your fabric piece and fold the top of the fabric down ¾" (1.9cm) so wrong sides are facing, and stitch a line across the fold at ⅛" (3mm). This is the same as a top stitch.

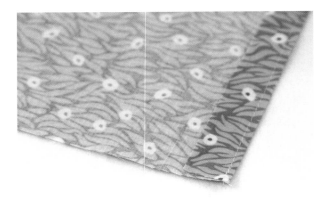

8. Unfold this first section, and then fold the fabric the same way 1" (2.5cm) apart and top stitch this next fold. The width will stay the same as the length of the fabric gets shorter.

9. Repeat step 8 until you have 4 stitched folds. Press toward the front.

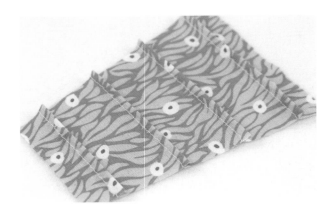

10. Using the lobster tail belly pattern piece, line up the seams with the lines and cut out the stitched fabric. Be gentle with this piece after cutting to avoid undoing all the top stitching, and set aside.

11. Sew all of the rear lobster fins (or flippers) by placing 2 like pieces right sides together, sewing around the curve from one corner to the other. Leave the flat edges open for turning. Notch the curved edges and turn each piece right side out.

12. Lay your fins out so the slanted longer pieces are on the outside, the shorter ones are on the inside and the pointed one is in the center.

13. Stack the fins the way you want to see them on your lobster tail. (I fussy cut many of the lobster pieces, and positioned the octopus part of the print on the center fin.) Pin fins together and set aside.

14. To start putting the tail together, sew the lobster inside tail pattern piece, right sides together, along the curved edge. Then notch the curved edge, which is now the center seam. NOTE: In a couple of these photos, you may notice I clipped when I should have notched. That's because I used to always clip everything, but now I know that not all curves work that way.

15. Open this piece, and place it right side down on top of the unpleated tail belly piece, which should be right side up. Find the center of the unpleated piece, and pin the front and back center seams to these marks.

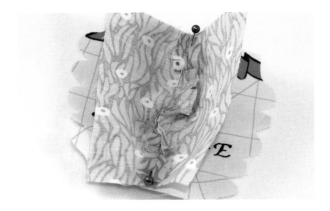

16. Sew the front edge of the inside tail piece ½" (1.3cm) in from the outside edges, down to the unpleated fabric underneath.

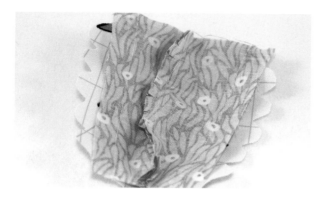

17. Turn this right side out and fold the curved edges inward to keep them from being sewn in the next step.

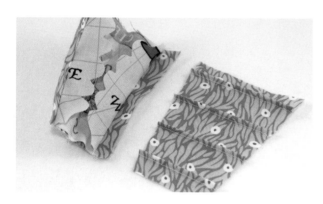

18. Lay the inside tail piece on top of the topstitched belly piece and sew the sides with a ¼" (6mm) seam allowance. Turn the pieces right side out.

19. Place the fins the same way you stacked them in step 13, down on top of the narrow end of the tail belly with raw edges aligned, and pin in place.

20. Flip this entire piece over on top of the pleated tail piece. Be sure to line up the front and back edges as well as the curves with each pleat.

21. Sew back from the top right corner, sewing each curve, along the back to sew in the fins, and up the other side along each curve. Use a smaller seam allowance (almost ⅛" [3mm]) in the tight curves, but the bottom flat edge should have a standard ¼" (6mm) seam allowance.

22. Cut and trim the excess fabric and carefully notch the outward curves and clip in between each curve.

23. Turn the entire tail right side out, carefully pushing out all the little curves, and set it aside.

ARMS/CLAWS

Make 2.

1. Cut out the lobster arm pattern pieces.

2. Begin by placing two lobster thumb pattern pieces right sides together, and sew from one side up to the tip and down the other. (Use an ⅛" [3mm] seam allowance.) Leave the flat edge open, and clip the edges. Turn and stuff.

3. Place the remaining lobster arm pattern pieces (claw, elbow and bicep) in the order they will be connected (see diagram).

4. Sew the bicep to the elbow with right sides together.

5. Sew the other edge of the elbow to the base of the claw with right sides together.

6. Position the thumb inward, and pin it so the raw edges are aligned and it lays on the inside of the claw, curved away from the elbow.

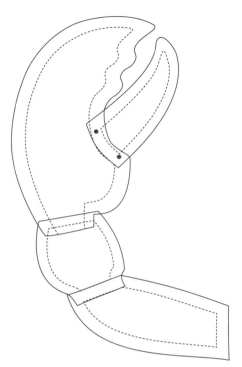

Placement of lobster arm pieces

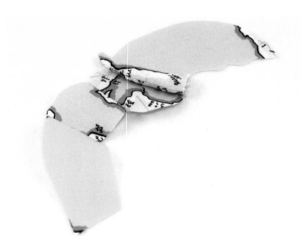

7. Repeat steps 3–5 to sew the underside of the lobster arm (without the thumb).

8. Lay the top of the lobster arm (right side facing down) on the underside of the lobster arm (right side facing up) and sew all the way around. Leave only the end of the bicep open for turning and stuffing.

9. Clip and notch all the way around the sewn arm, especially in the tight angles.

Tip For realistic lobster anatomy (one claw is always bigger than the other), you can adjust how open the claw is by placing the thumb in different positions, as well as making one claw smaller than the other by sewing a larger seam allowance to make it thinner. Do not make the elbow or biceps smaller, as they will then be very difficult to turn and stuff.

10. Turn the claw and arm right side out by tucking the tip of the lobster claw in a little first with the use of turning tools.

11. Pull the thumb out with the help of fabric tweezers. Be gentle to avoid ripping the thumb out.

12. Once the arm is turned out completely, carefully stuff the claw, elbow and bicep. Set aside.

ANTENNAE AND WALKING LEGS

1. Cut out the leg and antenna pattern pieces. With right sides facing together, sew each antenna up one side to the tip and down the other. They will need to be wide enough to fit your smallest turning tool, so adjust your seam allowance accordingly (approximately ⅛" [3mm]).

2. Turn each antenna right side out.

3. Place a pipe cleaner/chenille stem into each antenna. Bending and crimping the leading tip of the stick will prevent the metal from snagging the fabric and allow it to go in much smoother. The opposite end of the stick should be curled to hold it securely inside the lobster body.

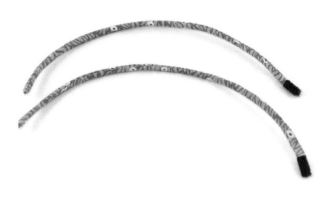

4. Prepare all the "walking" legs by sewing 2 leg pieces right sides together at a time, clipping and notching the edges, and turning them right side out. (These will also have smaller ⅛" (3mm) seam allowances and need to accommodate the smallest turning tool.)

5. Although it takes some time and patience, I prefer to stuff the legs, but that is optional. Be careful not to overstuff.

ASSEMBLING THE LOBSTER

1. Lay the lobster back pattern piece right side up. Pin an antenna, an arm and 4 legs to one side of the back piece. When placing the legs, have the first one near the arm, positioned so that the toe is pointing toward the front. The two middle legs are positioned so the toes are pointing up in the air, so they are sewn pointing downward. The last leg is positioned so the toe is pointing toward the back of the lobster.

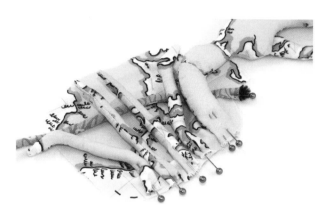

2. Now pin the other antenna, arm and 4 legs to the opposite side of the back piece.

3. Place the chest piece facedown over the back piece and sew up the sides so that the claws and legs are tucked into and dangling out of the chest cavity. The claws and legs should all be coming out the belly end; however, you can pull one of the claws up through the top for a little bit to have extra room. This is a challenging step, but don't be discouraged—it's worth it.

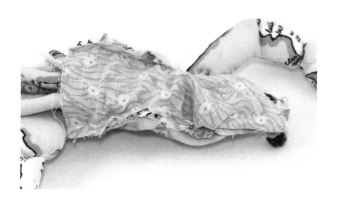

4. Once the second side is securely sewn most of the way up, tuck the arm/claw back down prior to sewing all the way up to the tip of the "nose."

5. After sewing the chest piece all the way to the tip, past the antennae, you should have a little leftover fabric from the back piece at the nose tip. If you notice on the pattern piece, the top of the back piece is a flat edge, about 1" (2.5cm) long. If you fold it in half, wrong sides together, you need to sew that ½" (1.3cm) edge closed, from the front fold to the chest piece connection. This is the nose.

6. Once the nose is sewn and all the antennae, arms and legs are secure, turn the lobster right side out. You now have the front half and the tail end of the lobster.

7. Flip the tail on top of the lobster's back so that the raw edges align. Make sure the center of the back and tail are aligned and pin in place. The side seams will not match up because the tail is wider and will curl around toward the belly; however, you can still make sure the sides are equally spaced.

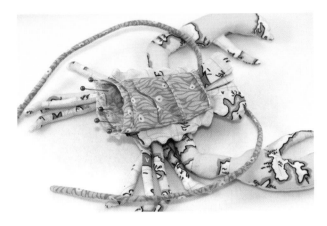

8. Sew as much of the "waist" as you can from one side seam of the back to the other, so you have less to hand sew on the belly.

9. Flip the tail back down after sewing and stuff the chest cavity and the tail to the desired fullness, through the opening between the belly and the tail.

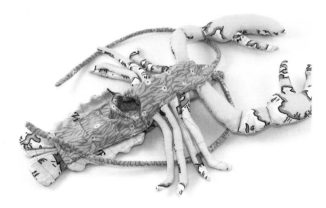

10. Close the belly seam using a ladder stitch.

11. Add some eyes if you'd like, using a needle and embroidery floss (see page 17) or nice round beads (see page 16).

Bob the Buoy

My name is Bob and I am a buoy. I spent many years off the coast of Greenport, floating and bobbing up and down with the tide. Early in the morning, the lobstermen always came looking for me. I would call out, "Here I am, over here." They always heard me and would come closer, then carefully pull me out of the water. I was attached to a big wooden trap and would help them catch lobsters to eat. When they were done emptying the trap, they would toss it and me back into the water, while asking me to "keep an eye on that trap for us," so I did.

After many years of wind, rain and sun, I was pulled from the water one last time. My job was done, so I retired and am now proudly on display with all my old friends.

Retired buoys are a common sight in many coastal towns, displayed on lobster shacks or mailboxes. Make a few for your bed or couch, or a wall full of them. Either way, you won't be able to resist getting creative with numerous color combinations.

FINISHED LENGTH: Varies depending on number and width of fabric strips used; shown range from 21½" (54.6cm) with pole to 10" (25.4cm) without pole

SUPPLIES

Templates (page 119) • Fabric: ½ yard (.5m), or 2–3 fat quarters (for variations) per buoy • Stuffing • 5' (1.5m) polyester rope (from hardware store) per buoy (optional) • Thread • Basic sewing tools (pages 8–10)

FABRICS SHOWN: solids courtesy FreeSpirit/Westminster Fibers Fabric

Tip This pattern offers a lot of creative license. You can choose your colors, add length to the buoy, add the pole or use only a rope, or do both. You get to decide the end result. In Maine most buoys have a pole on one end, maybe even on both ends, because the poles make it easier to grab the buoys out of the water.

INSTRUCTIONS

1. Begin by cutting long strips of fabric (up to 22" [56cm] long) in widths of your choice (cut on the crosswise grain so the strips stretch a little). I use 5" (12.7cm), 4" (10.1cm) and 3" (7.6cm) wide strips. Variety is good, so feel free to mix it up and use other widths, too.

2. Sew the long edges of the strips together with right sides facing. Sew as many or as few as you want. Create a pattern or make it random.

3. After sewing the strips together, flip them over and press the seams toward the darker color.

Tip If you are using white or lighter colors with darker colors, press the seam allowance toward the darker color, otherwise the seam allowance will show through the lighter fabric once stuffed and finished.

4. Optional: Sew a top stitch to hold down the seam allowance to prevent it from moving while stuffing. Make it contrasting, or use like colors.

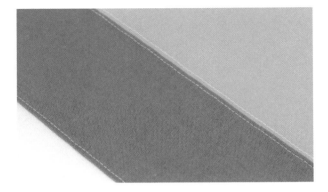

5. Fold the sewn panel in half, then in half again, lining up the seams so all pieces are cut straight. Pin the buoy pattern on top and cut out the 4 pattern pieces.

6. Lay 2 pieces of the buoy right sides together and sew the side edge from the end up to the middle of the tip. Be sure to line up the seams.

Tip If adding rope, do not sew all the way up to the tip. Leave at least ¼" (6mm) or ½" (1.3cm), depending on the thickness of the rope (see "To add rope to the top" steps on page 66).

7. Open them up, and with right sides together, sew another section of the buoy to one of the first pieces.

8. Open the fabric up these 3 panels and sew the last panel onto the third panel.

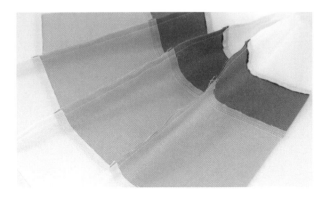

9. Connect the first and last panels, right sides together, and sew the edge, leaving at least 2" (5.1cm) open in the middle of the buoy edge for turning and stuffing. Set the buoy aside to make the pole. (NOTE: If you are not adding a pole, skip to the "To use rope only (no pole)" section on page 66.)

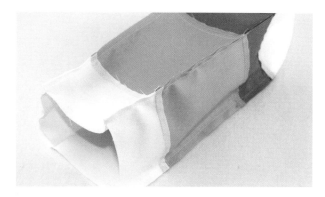

TO ADD A POLE (OPTIONAL)

1. Cut the buoy pole pattern piece and fold it in half lengthwise (so it's long and skinny) with right sides together. Sew the long edge together.

2. Press one end of the pole so you have 4 creases: one on the top and bottom, and both sides.

3. Fold the buoy pole tip pattern piece in half and then in half again, and press. Line up these 4 crease marks with the ones on the pole end, right sides together, and pin in place. Then pin in between.

4. Sew all the way around and remove the pins.

5. Notch around the curved edge of the pole end, and turn right side out.

6. Cut the buoy base pattern piece and fold the circle in half, and then in half again. Cut out the center. Do not cut extra or it will get too big and stretched out.

7. Press the folds on the buoy base and also on the end of the pole.

8. Place the inside cutout of the base around the exterior of the buoy pole, right sides together, to match up the creases, then pin in place.

9. Sew all the way around the inside of the base center and remove the pins.

10. Place the pole inside the buoy, which is still turned inside out, so right sides are facing.

11. Line up the creases on the base with the seams on the buoy, then pin and sew in place.

12. Clip or notch around the edge of the base, the inside of the base, and on the curved tip of the buoy.

13. Begin turning the buoy right side out by gently pulling the pole out through the opening, then turning the entire buoy right side out.

14. Stuff your buoy pole and then the buoy to the desired firmness, and close with a ladder stitch.

TO ADD ROPE TO THE TOP

1. If you want to add a rope through the top of the buoy, simply do not sew the last ¼" (6mm) to ½" (1.3cm) at the pointed tip of the buoy.

2. Before turning the buoy right side out, place the end of the rope through the side opening and the tip opening, so about 1" (2.5cm) is sticking out.

3. Hand-sew a back stitch all the way around the tip, through the fabric and through the rope.

4. To strengthen the connection, put the needle through the rope from one side to the other a few times before tying a knot.

5. Pull the rope and tip of the buoy through the opening to turn right side out, and finish with step 14 of the previous section.

TO USE ROPE ONLY (NO POLE)

1. Cut out the buoy base pattern piece and fold the circle in quarters. Press or crease the edges and center. Cut a small plus sign into the center (very small, as it will stretch easily).

2. Match up the outer crease marks to the buoy seams, then pin and sew in place (buoy should still be right side out).

3. Place the rope through the side opening and through the top so that the amount coming out of the top is long enough to pass through the buoy once turned right side out, with at least 10" (25cm) to spare for tying a knot underneath, and with about 3½' (1.1m) of hanging rope at the top.

4. Follow steps 3–4 in the "To add rope to the top" section.

5. Before turning right side out through the side opening, notch the fabric around the curved tip of the buoy and the base edge. Once turned right side out, the shorter length of the rope should be on the inside of the buoy, coming straight down (and out of) the small center on the base.

6. Stuff the buoy starting at the top first, making sure to keep the rope in the center.

7. With a hidden backstitch, hand-sew the base of the buoy to the rope.

8. Tie a knot in the rope under the base of the stuffed buoy. Sew the side of the buoy closed with a ladder stitch.

Casco the Dolphin

asco is a one-year-old bottle-nosed dolphin born last summer at a nearby aquarium. He loves to do tricks. His two favorites are jumping through hoops and pushing balls down under the water. He tries hard to swim up and break the surface of the water before the ball pops back up. If he beats the ball, Casco gets an extra fish treat each time, and he loves fish!

Today, Casco and his mommy will be released back into the vast wild ocean where they belong. His mommy was injured when she was caught in a fisherman's net. Soon after arriving at the aquarium to get better, she had Casco. He's a little nervous to venture outside of the aquarium, but excited to explore new places and make new friends on the ocean floor.

This pattern is so easy and quick, you'll want to make a whole pod of dolphins! Make one to play with, or make a larger one to cuddle with.

FINISHED LENGTH: 6" (15.2cm) and 10" (25.4cm)

SUPPLIES

Templates (page 120) • Fabric: 1 fat quarter, or 2 for variety (makes both Casco and mama) • Stuffing • Thread • Basic sewing tools (pages 8–10)

FABRIC SHOWN: from the Kaffe Fassett Classics collection, courtesy Rowan/Westminster Fibers Fabric

INSTRUCTIONS

1. Trace and cut out the dolphin pattern pieces using the fabrics of your choice.

2. Place the dolphin side pieces right sides together and sew the spine from the nose, around the dorsal fin and to the tail, then set aside.

3. Take 2 fin pieces and sew them right sides together, then repeat for the second fin.

4. Clip or notch the edges carefully and turn the fins right side out.

5. Place the dolphin belly pieces right sides together and sew on the straight edge from the nose toward the belly about 2" (5.1cm), or 4" (10.2cm) for mama. Then sew from the tail to the belly about 1½" (3.8cm), or 3½" (8.9cm) for mama. This will leave an opening approximately 2" (5.1cm), or 3" (7.6cm) for mama, in the center for turning and stuffing.

NOTE: If you do not want your dolphin to be a finger puppet, then sew up this seam without leaving an opening and skip steps 6–8.

6. Take the finger pouch pieces and place them right sides together. Fold ¼" (6mm) of the flat edge on only the top piece, and leave the other edge unfolded.

7. Sew from one corner around the finger shape to the other corner, leaving the flat edge open.

8. Place the raw flat edge of the unfolded finger piece to the flat edge opening of the belly, right sides facing. Sew this piece in place on only one side. It will not be connected to the other side until the very end, when the belly is closed after stuffing.

9. Pin the raw edge of the fins on the outside edge of the belly pieces so that the top of the fin is 2" (5.1cm) from the nose tip, or 4" (10.2cm) for mama, and the tips of the fins are pointing down toward the tail.

10. With the belly pieces right side up, place the top of the dolphin right side down. Line up the seams and pin the nose and the tail in place.

11. Sew the dolphin all the way around from the tip of the nose, around the body and back to the nose.

12. Clip or notch all of the edges, and around the tail and the upper fin.

13. Carefully turn the fins right side out and then the nose of the dolphin.

14. Pull the finger pouch out of the inside to keep it out of the way.

15. Stuff the dolphin's nose, upper dorsal fin and tail first. Then stuff the body. Do not overstuff, or the finger pouch will be impossible to use.

16. Poke the finger pouch back into the dolphin, making sure it's not in a bunch.

17. Close the opening by using a ladder stitch. First close one end. When you reach the finger pouch, only sew the edge of the dolphin to the unsewn edge of the pouch. Then sew the other end past the finger edge to close the belly completely.

3

Arctic Adventures

Every summer, my daughters and I head south to visit my twin sister and her boys. While the temperature soars outside, the air conditioning inside keeps us cool enough to need coats! My nephews inspired this section with their wild and imaginative adventures in their own Arctic world.

Bear Buddies: SNOWFLAKE & ANGEL

Snowflake and Angel are playing around and enjoying the first feeling of snow on their paws. They are as white as the snow around them, and from a distance they are hard to see because they are so small. Sometimes they look a little bluish, like the ice, because of their special fur.

These silly little polar bears love to play hide-and-seek in the snow while their mama is off searching for food to feed them after a long winter's nap. They try to stay very quiet like Mama told them to, but sometimes they call out for her because they miss her while she's gone. Good thing they have each other for company until she returns!

These polar bear cubs can fit into your child's backpack or pocket. They will go anywhere you want them to, and keep a little one happily occupied when bored. Make them an igloo to play in, and they will have hours of fun together.

FINISHED LENGTH: 4½" (11.5cm)

SUPPLIES

Templates (page 121) • Fabric: 1 fat eighth (per cub) • Stuffing • Embroidery floss • Thread • Basic sewing tools (pages 8–10)

FABRIC SHOWN: from the Pretty Little Things collection by Dena Designs, courtesy FreeSpirit/ Westminster Fibers Fabric

INSTRUCTIONS

1. Cut out the polar bear pattern pieces using the fabric of your choice.

2. Sew both of the ears, the legs and the tail by placing 2 like pieces right sides together, sewing from one end around to the other end and leaving the flat edges open for turning.

3. Clip or notch all of the edges and curves, being careful not to clip the seams.

4. Using a turning tool, turn all of these pieces right side out.

5. Stuff the legs to the desired fullness, but do not over-stuff.

6. Place one of the belly pieces right side up.

7. Place an arm with a curved end on top of the belly piece, right sides together, aligning the curved raw edges and sew in place.

8. Repeat step 7 with the other arm and belly piece.

9. Place both belly pieces right sides together, and sew the center edges from the top to the bottom.

10. Pin the tail in place on the right side of one back body piece. It can be laid flat or folded (as shown) to lay more accurately, as a polar bear's tail would lay.

11. Place the other back body piece right side facing on top, and sew the back spine together.

12. Open the back piece and line up the back of the arms with the straight edge using the front belly pattern piece as your guide. Pin the arm pieces in place. Remove the front belly pattern piece used for reference.

13. Sew the back arm pieces in place to the sides of the back.

14. Pin the legs in place ⅝" (1.6cm) away from the center of the bottom seam, so the legs are pointing in toward the tail and the raw edges are lined up.

15. With the back of the polar bear cub pieced and pinned together, place the front of the polar bear cub on top and pin in place with right sides together.

Tip Pin the arms first, then the neck, bottom center seams and armpits, and anywhere else necessary.

16. Sew from one side of the neck all the way around the entire bear to the other side of the neck. Leave the neck open for turning and stuffing.

17. Place a side head piece right side up and place the top head piece right side down and sideways on top. Sew the face seam together.

18. Open these two pieces and place the other side head piece on the opposite side of the top head piece.

19. Sew the other face seam together.

20. Fold the face in half, right sides together, and sew the two pieces from the bottom of the neck up to the bridge of the nose.

21. There will be a tiny hole in the tip of the nose, which needs to be closed. Flatten the underside of the nose seam and sew straight across the top of the nose tip.

22. Flip over the face of the polar bear and pin the ears to the top of the head, centering each one at the top seams.

23. Sew both back head pieces right sides together, from the top to the bottom.

24. Open the back head pieces and pin the back, right sides facing, to the front head pieces.

25. Sew from one corner of the neck up the side of the head and around to the other side, then down to the base of the neck.

26. Clip or notch all of the sewn edges on the head and then turn the head right side out.

27. Clip or notch all the sewn edges on the body, including the armpits and just above the arms as well, and then turn the body right side out.

28. Gently stuff the polar bear head and body.

29. Sew the head to the body using a ladder stitch all the way around the neck. To make this process easier, take a fabric marker and draw a ¼" (6mm) seam allowance to guide you.

30. Sew on eyes using embroidery floss (see page 17), and use basic stitching to add a nose.

BooBoo the Igloo

Here in the Arctic Circle, there are days when the sun never rises. It's dark and cold all winter long, but I, BooBoo the Igloo, am here. Enter my doorway, and I will be your shelter and keep you warm. We can share stories, crochet cozy sweaters and wait patiently for the sun to rise once again.

When the sun at last breaks over the horizon, everything will spring to life. Fold me up, and I will travel with you as you go hunting for food. We must go before the ice melts on the river. Be on the lookout for bears; they will be waking up now, and they will be hungry, too. Come inside and I will keep you hidden and safe.

Many Arctic adventures await in this reversible igloo that is easy to make. Setup and take-down is a breeze too, so take it with you wherever you go. It's perfect for a child's favorite toy, doll or animal. You can even make one for your own small pet.

FINISHED HEIGHT: 6¾" (17.1cm)

SUPPLIES

Templates (page 122) • Fabric: ½ yard (.5m) each of 2 different patterns • 3 poles: heavy-duty ¼" (6mm) zip ties or ¼" (6mm) poly tubing • 8" (20.3cm) of ¼" (6mm) ribbon • 6" × 5" (15.2cm × 12.7cm) piece of heavyweight stabilizer • Thread • Basic sewing tools (pages 8–10)

FABRICS SHOWN: from the Field Study collection by Anna Maria Horner, courtesy FreeSpirit/Westminster Fibers Fabric

IGLOO DOME

1. Cut out all the igloo pattern pieces using the fabric of your choice.

2. If using long strips (or width) of fabric, cut 2 strips that are 2½" × 24" (6.4cm × 61cm) long to make the igloo pole tabs. If using scraps, cut out all 24 of your tab pieces to 2½" × 1½" (6.4cm × 3.8cm).

3. Place the strips right sides together and sew both edges of the longest length. (NOTE: If sewing with scrap pieces, sew the shorter length edges. You can save time sewing the scrap pieces by strip-piecing [see page 12]. You still need to lock in your beginning and ending stitch on each piece, so they don't tear apart when turning.)

4. Turn the strip (or pieces) right side out and press.

5. Top stitch the same seams that were sewn previously.

6. If you sewed a strip, cut the strip into 1½" (3.8cm) wide pieces. Either way, you should have 12 finished tabs with a top stitch along the short edges. The long sides should be raw edges, as they will be sewn into the igloo panel seams. Set these tabs aside.

7. Cut 6 pieces of fabric for your pole base ends that are 3½" × 1½" (8.9cm × 3.8cm) each. Lay each piece right side up, fold it in half and stitch the short ends together.

8. Fold the piece in half again so the folded edge lines up with the stitched seam (as shown at left below), not the raw edge. Fold the seam allowance under and stitch only one end closed (as shown at right below).

9. Turn right side out. Repeat steps 7–9 for the other 5 pole base ends, so you have 6 total.

10. Align 2 of the Fabric B igloo panels (the side that will not have tabs), right sides together, and place 1 panel of Fabric A directly on top of the 2 Fabric B panels, right side up.

11. Place and pin a pole base end piece at least ⅜" (10mm) away from the bottom edge of the panels lined up on the right edge.

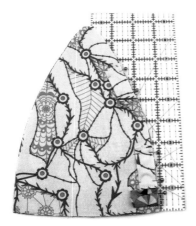

12. Fold the pole tabs in half lengthwise so that the raw edges line up.

13. Place and pin 2 pole tabs on the right side of the panel also, so that the bottom of 1 tab is approximately 1" (2.5cm) up from the bottom, and the second tab is lined up 5" (12.7cm) from the bottom. See the pattern piece for placement details if necessary.

14. Once all tabs are pinned, cover the panels and tabs with another panel of Fabric A, right side down.

15. Sew only the right side from the bottom, all the way to the center of the top. Notch the sewn edge before proceeding.

Tip If you do not sew far enough into the center of the tip, the igloo top will have a hole in the center, which will be difficult to close.

16. Open the fabric panels so that both Fabric A panels are right side up and both Fabric B panels are right side down. All of the tabs should be in between your Fabric A panels.

17. Place a panel of Fabric B right side up, underneath the panels on the right side, not the left.

18. Place the pole base end and pole tabs again along the right side as you did previously in steps 11–13.

19. Place a panel of Fabric A, right side down, on top of the right side panels.

20. Sew the right side edge again as you did in step 15.

21. Repeat steps 16–20 until you have 5 sections of the igloo top all sewn together. Set this aside to make the doorway.

IGLOO DOORWAY

1. Place the long doorway pieces right sides together and the long doorway stabilizer piece on top.

2. Sew along the longest straight edge (which will be the front edge) of the doorway arch.

3. Place the doorway base pieces with the right sides together and the doorway base stabilizer piece on top.

4. Sew along the longest straight edge (which will be the front edge) of the doorway base.

5. Open both the doorway piece and the base, and match up like fabrics, with right sides together. Pin one side of the doorway to one side of the base, and then pin the other side so it looks like a tunnel.

6. Sew both pinned edges and turn the fabric pieces without the stabilizer over on top of the stabilizer pieces, so the doorway is right side out and reversible.

7. Line up the raw edges of the doorway and pin together.

8. Take the last two igloo panels (1 of Fabric A, 1 of Fabric B) and cut out the doorway opening in each.

9. Pin one igloo panel doorway, right sides facing, to the doorway arch (match up like fabrics if you prefer).

10. Flip the pieces to the reverse side, and then pin the other igloo panel to the doorway in the same way.

11. Sew from the bottom of one side up and around the arch of the doorway to the other side, and down to the bottom.

12. Lay the doorway panel down so Fabric A is right side up (Fabric B will be right side down).

13. Place the final pole base ends and pole tabs to the right and left side, using the same measurements as all the others.

IGLOO ASSEMBLY

1. Take the 5 panels that are connected and place them with Fabric A side up. Flip the sixth doorway panel face-down on top and pin the Fabric A panels to the doorway panel.

2. Sew both pinned edges from the bottom up to the center of the top.

3. The outside (Fabric A) of the igloo is all sewn together, but the reverse side is not. Connect 2 of the Fabric B panels right sides together. In order to do this, you will have to wrap up the whole igloo in a pocket.

4. You won't be able to get all the way to the top; however, sew from the bottom up to the top as far as you can go without sewing any other panels into the seam.

5. Pull the whole igloo out of the pocket, and now repeat steps 3–4 to sew the last 2 panels together. This will look the same as step 4.

6. After you pull the igloo out of the pocket again, all the pieces will be connected. However, the top of the reverse side (Fabric B) will need to be sewn together at the top by hand. Using a ladder stitch, sew the 2 seams up to the top center to close.

7. Place 1 piece of the base right side up and pin the bottom raw edge of the igloo dome all the way around the raw edge of the base.

8. Place the other base piece right side down on top of the igloo dome and re-pin all layers in place.

9. Starting ½" (1.3cm) from the inside of the doorway base seam, sew all the way around the base of the igloo just past ½" (1.3cm) of the other side of the doorway base seam, leaving approximately 2" (5.1cm) open for turning.

10. Notch the edge all the way around the base.

11. Gently pull the igloo through the opening to turn it right side out.

12. Using a ladder stitch, sew the opening closed.

13. Hand-stitch an 8" (20.3cm) piece of ribbon to the top center of the igloo on the tab side (Fabric A).

14. To make the poles, trim your ¼" (6mm) poly tubing or heavy-duty zip ties to size. This may require using a pocket blade or small knife, so only adults should do it. NOTE: When reversing the igloo, there will be less room inside for the poles, so those poles will need to be cut shorter than the outside ones. So, trim your zip ties to 19" (48.3cm) for the outside and 18" (46cm) for the inside. If you are using tubing, they will cross over each other and each one will have to be a slightly different length, starting at 19" (48.3cm) and going up in ⅜" (1cm) increments: 19⅜" (49.2cm) and 19¾" (50.2cm).

15. Place all 3 poles in through the pole tabs all the way across to the opposite side of the dome. Each pole should pass through 4 tabs.

16. Place the ends of the poles into their appropriate pole ends, measure the poles one at a time accordingly, trim any excess, and then place the opposite ends into the appropriate pole tabs. Tie ribbon up and over the poles to secure.

Drifter the Orca Whale

Beep-beep-whistle, click-click-ting. I'm an orca whale, and that's how we talk to each other. We are gathering our families together to travel up to the Bering Sea. We love to swim and rarely ever sleep. I'm Drifter, and I was born two years ago off the coast of Tonga. When the water gets warm down here in the Southern Hemisphere, we have to travel north where the water is still cold.

I hope to live a long life like my grandma—she is almost fifty years old! She doesn't really look like me, because we all have different markings on our bodies. None of us look alike at all, really, except that we are all black, white and gray. I hope you'll join us on our journey!

My daughter made an orca whale for her first diorama project in the second grade. She wanted to make a stuffie to go with it. I helped modify her first pattern, and she sewed some of it with me on the machine and then did all the rest herself by hand. This is a great first project, as easy as it is fun.

FINISHED LENGTH: 6" (15.2cm) and 7" (17.8cm)

SUPPLIES

Templates (page 121) • Fat quarter fabrics: 2 black, 1 white and 1 gray, or desired colors/patterns (yields 4 orcas) • Stuffing • Clear fishing line and bead (optional) • Seam sealant (such as Fray Block) (optional) • Thread • Basic sewing tools (pages 8–10)

FABRICS SHOWN: solids courtesy FreeSpirit/Westminster Fibers Fabric

INSTRUCTIONS

1. Cut out all the orca whale pattern pieces for each orca using the fabric of your choice. The steps that follow show Orca A. (If you want to get creative, use different solid-colored fabric or patterns.) Orca B can be sewn using the same steps that follow, using Fin B pieces accordingly.

2. Place the Orca A whale pieces right sides together, and sew from the nose up over the spine and all the way around the tail flukes. Just after sewing the tail flukes, stop to leave room for the belly piece. Lock in your stitches.

3. Take 2 Fin A pieces and sew them right sides together, and repeat with the other 2 A pieces, leaving the flat edges open for turning.

4. Clip or notch around the sewn edges of the fins and carefully turn the fins right side out.

5. Pin the fins on the inside edges, just forward of the dorsal fin alignment.

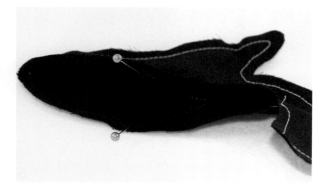

6. Pin the front center of the belly to the seam of the nose, and pin the belly to both edges.

7. Sew one side of the belly from the top of the nose and down to the end of the belly piece.

8. Sew the other side of the belly from the top of the nose to just past the fin. Lock in the stitch, leave a 1½" (3.8cm) opening (for turning and stuffing), and then sew the last ¾" (1.9cm) end of the belly piece.

9. Carefully clip or notch all the edges without clipping the seams.

10. Turn the orca whale right side out, using a turning tool if necessary.

11. Gently stuff the tail flukes first, then the dorsal fin, and finish from the nose into the center.

> *Tip* A whole pod of these orca whales would make a perfect baby mobile.

12. Cut 2 identical white patches for the eyes, 2 other white patches for the sides (optional; not shown), and 1 piece of gray, folded fabric to use as the patch for the back, behind the fin. Orcas are very symmetrical, so drawing a pattern piece first, folding, and then cutting will keep it accurate.

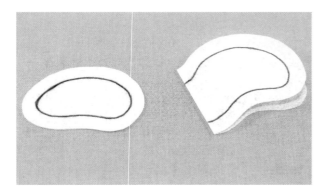

Tip Because all orca whales have different markings, there are no pattern pieces for the eye, side and back patches. This will keep them unique; however, you should use scraps of pattern paper pieces to create them prior to cutting the fabric, to keep them symmetrical.

13. Place the patches in their proper location, and sew each one in place using the stitch of your choice by placing the threaded needle through the opening to hide the thread ends. I have used a blanket stitch to keep the edges secured, which will help prevent some fraying. You can also use a seam sealant to prevent fraying during this step.

14. If your orca whale will hang in a baby mobile, diorama or from anywhere else, tie a small bead onto a long fishing line, and insert the needle and line through the opening before closing it. Pull the needle and line out from where you want it to hang. (If you want the orca to pitch forward, the fishing line should come out from the top of the dorsal fin, or behind the fin. If you want it to pitch upward, the line should come out in front of the dorsal fin.)

15. Once all the patches are sewn on, close the belly opening with a ladder stitch.

Mimi the Hot-Air Balloon

U p, up and away, through the clouds and over the vast Arctic lands. Hop into my basket and I will carry you on a swift cool breeze. You will see the world from way up high, and as we ascend, the clouds will get bigger and bigger, and the world below will get smaller and smaller. No need to be afraid. I am Mimi the Hot-Air Balloon, and I have sailed on these Arctic breezes for many years, loving every ride.

On a beautiful day like today, we will soar with the birds in the sky. Can you feel the excitement? If you release sand from my bags, we will rise even higher. Do you see the mountains in the distance or the deep blue ocean? Do you see the mama polar bear and her cubs roaming around on the sheets of ice? Come and float away with me, and the magic will last a lifetime.

Make your own hot-air balloon to float away on. Fussy cut the fabric to make a pattern so spectacular that you will want to make many more. Hang it in a window or anywhere you like. The basket can even hold a small friend for the ride.

FINISHED HEIGHT: 13" (33cm) with basket

SUPPLIES

Templates (page 123) • Fabric: ¼ yard (.3m) each of 2 or more patterns, or ½ yard (.5m) each if fussy cutting • Stuffing (a bamboo or dense fiber is not recommended) • 3" (7.6cm) square scrap piece of heavyweight stabilizer • 20" (50.8cm) of decorative string • Thread • Basic sewing tools (pages 8–10)

FABRICS SHOWN: from the Alchemy collection by Amy Butler, courtesy Rowan/Westminster Fibers Fabric

BALLOON

1. Cut out all the balloon pattern pieces. If you choose to fussy cut your fabrics to maximize the design, you will need extra fabric. Although this pattern is not reversible once stuffed, the inside of the balloon will be visible. So you can use regular fabric or muslin if you'd like.

Tip The hot-air balloon is constructed similarly to the igloo dome pattern on pages 77–78.

2. To begin sewing the balloon, first layer 2 Pattern A pieces with right sides facing, and then on top of that, 2 Pattern B pieces with right sides facing. In the photo they are fanned out to show the order, but make sure your pieces are all stacked neatly.

3. Sew one long edge from the bottom of the pieces all the way up to the middle of the top edge.

4. Notch the curved edge you just sewed without clipping the seam.

Tip Although you would normally clip or notch around all edges after you have completed sewing, with this pattern you will need to clip or notch these edges as you go along.

5. Fold over the top piece and the bottom piece and line up the edges. You should now see all right sides up on top and right sides down on the reverse.

6. If you have 2 distinct patterns, be sure to match your patterns as you lay the next piece of Pattern A right side down on top, and Pattern B right side facing up on the reverse side.

7. Sew the outer edge from the bottom of the pieces all the way up to the middle of the top, and then notch the sewn edge without clipping the seam, as you did in steps 3–4.

8. Open up the top and bottom pieces by folding them over to the left or right side depending on which side you just stitched. You should now have 3 segments connected.

9. The balloon is made up of 6 total segments. Continue sewing the next 3 segments by following steps 5–8.

10. When all of the segments are connected, you will need to connect the first segment to the last segment. Before connecting them, decide which side you want facing outward when the balloon is all done.

11. The side you want facing out should be on the inside during this step. Place both edges together, so the right sides are facing. You will only sew 3 of the 4 segment pieces together along the outer edge from the bottom to the middle of the top (one piece from your second chosen fabric will be left out).

12. Take the last piece that was not sewn and wrap it around the whole balloon, so it envelops the entire top.

13. Sew the bottom edge approximately 3" (7.6cm) up along the side.

14. Leave a 2" (5.1cm) opening, and then sew the remaining top edge closed, as far up to the tip as you can. Due to the bulk of the fabric on the inside, you will not be able to sew all the way up.

15. Clip or notch this edge all the way up, except for the single piece in the opening section.

16. Carefully turn the balloon right side out, turning the bottom out through the side opening first before turning the rest.

17. Using a ladder stitch, close the opening on the side.

18. Using a ladder stitch, close the opening on the top as well and turn the balloon right side out, so the side you wanted facing out is now showing.

19. Each segment of the balloon will need to be stuffed through its own channel opening at the bottom. Stuff a little bit into each segment at a time, working your way around the balloon. As you are stuffing, it will want to slide down from the top; continue to push it back up each time and eventually it will stay.

20. Once you have stuffed each segment, take the base bands, fold each of them right sides together and sew the short ends together. Turn 1 right side out, and keep 1 right side in.

21. Line up 1 base band, wrong side out, along the out-side of the balloon base, and pin in place at each seam.

22. Place the other base band on the inside of the balloon, right sides facing. Re-pin all layers together.

23. Unless you have an industrial sewing machine with the right height, it will be easier to hand sew all these layers together along the raw edge.

24. Once sewn, fold down the base bands. Fold a single hem on the raw edges toward the inside of each other and pin them together. Place 4 pins evenly spaced: 2 should be in the seams of the segments, across from each other; the other 2 should be in the middle of the segments. (It won't be exact, because there are only 6 segments instead of 8.) These 4 locations will connect the strings from the balloon to the 4 corners of the basket.

25. Cut 4 pieces of decorative string that are 3" (7.6cm) long. Tie a knot on both ends of each piece, and place 1 piece of string in between the 2 base pieces, where each pin was placed.

26. Top stitch the edge of the band, sewing the string into the seam.

BASKET

1. To make the basket, begin by stacking the following pieces: 2 Pattern A pieces with right sides facing, 1 piece of heavyweight stabilizer on top of those, and 2 Pattern B pieces with right sides facing on top of the stabilizer.

2. Sew only 1 edge with inset seams. Leave ¼" (6mm) open at the 2 corners.

3. Open the Pattern B piece on top, and open the Pattern A piece underneath, on the bottom.

4. Place another Pattern B piece on top, right side down, and a Pattern A piece underneath, right side up.

5. Sew only 1 edge, with inset seams, opposite from the first seam. You should now have the base in the center, and 2 sides attached, on top and bottom.

6. Fold the top pieces diagonally to reveal a top edge that has not been sewn yet, and fold the pieces underneath in the same way to reveal the same top edge.

7. Place a Pattern B piece on top, right side down, and a Pattern A piece underneath, right side up.

8. Sew all the way across the top edge. You can sew with inset seams, but you don't have to. Open up all the pieces on the top and the bottom.

9. Repeat steps 6–8 to the final edge.

10. Open all the pieces. The top side should look just like the underside with all right sides out, and the center is the only piece with stabilizer.

11. Begin sewing 2 of the side seams, right sides together, on the Pattern B side. Start at the top edge and sew down to the base so that the top edges remain even.

12. Continue to sew each edge together, repeating step 11 until all sides are sewn together to make an open basket.

13. Repeat this process on the reverse side with fabric Pattern A.

14. Whichever side of the basket you want facing out, pull that side up and over the other side, after carefully clipping the corners to reduce bulk.

15. Just as you did on the base of the balloon, fold a single hem on the raw edges of the basket toward the inside, and pin each corner seam.

SANDBAGS

Sandbags are optional. You can make as few or as many as you'd like, or none at all. If you do not want to make any, skip this section.

1. Take a piece of the sandbag fabric and fold it in half with right sides facing.

2. Tuck the fold up into the center so that there is an ⅛" (3mm) fold tucked inside. (This will be the bottom.)

3. Sew the side edges and then clip with pinking shears.

4. Turn the sandbag right side out and stuff gently.

5. Before sewing the top edge closed, use pinking shears again to clip the top edge to prevent fraying.

6. Cut a 3" (7.6cm) piece of decorative string, place a knot in each end, and stick one end into the top of the sandbag.

7. Sew the top of the sandbag closed.

8. Place the opposite end of the sandbag string in between the 2 fabric pieces of the basket. You can place them near the corner seams or in the middle of the sides.

BALLOON ASSEMBLY

1. Place the ends of the strings on the balloon into the corners of the basket and pin in place.

2. Top stitch around the top edge of the basket. You may have to lift your sewing foot and reposition the pieces more than once, to avoid sewing the strings down or getting them all caught up.

3. To finish your hot-air balloon, you need a loop to hang it with. Cut a circle of fabric at least 1½" (3.8cm) wide—you choose the size; this can be based on fussy cutting a piece of the fabric pattern (as shown)—and a piece of heavyweight stabilizer that is ½" (1.3cm) smaller in width than the fabric.

4. Wrap the fabric around the stabilizer and thread your string through the center top of the fabric and the stabilizer, and then double knot the string on the inside.

5. Stitch this loop piece to the top center of your hot-air balloon.

4

A Rainy Day

No matter how many gray clouds hang in the sky or how many drops of rain fill nearby puddles, these pretty patterns are sure to brighten any rainy day.

Dolly Moses Basket

The sun is up, little dolly, rise and shine. Let's go outside to play. We can lay your blanket out on the pretty grass and have a tea party picnic. When the tea and cookies are all gone, I will read you a book and you can play with your tiny toes.

Come little dolly, it's getting darker outside and it's time to go to sleep. I'll place you in your cozy bed and wrap you tight and warm. You can rest your precious head on your pillow, and I will sing you a song until your eyes grow heavy. Goodnight, dolly. Sweet dreams. Sleep tight. I love you.

This reversible pattern with quilt and pillow can be adjusted to fit any size doll or stuffed animal. This basket is not suitable for use with a real baby.

FINISHED BASKET LENGTH: varies; small 10" (25.4cm), medium 13" (33cm) or large 18" (45.7cm)

SUPPLIES

Templates (page 123) • Fabric: *(small set)* ⅔ yard (.6m) each of 2 patterns, or *(medium set)* 1 yard (.9m) each, or *(large set)* 1½ yards (1.4m) each; 1–2 additional fat quarters for variety in pillow or quilt (optional) • Warm & Natural cotton batting: *(small set)* ¾ yard (.7m), *(medium set)* 1 yard (.9m) or *(large set)* 1½ yards (1.4m) • Heavyweight stabilizer: *(small set)* 1 fat eighth or *(medium or large set)* 1 fat quarter • Stuffing (for pillow) • Thread • Basic sewing tools (pages 8–10)

FABRICS SHOWN: from The Birds and the Bees collection by Tula Pink, courtesy FreeSpirit/Westminster Fibers Fabric

CUTTING (FOR BASKET)

Basket base templates are provided for 3 basket sizes. Below are cutting guidelines for the rim (sides) and handles. For the rim, cut 1 each for Fabric A, Fabric B and the batting. For the handles, cut 2 each for Fabric A, Fabric B and the batting.

For a small basket, cut: 5" × 30" (12.7cm × 76.2cm) rim; 2" × 10" (5.1cm × 25.4cm) handles

For a medium basket, cut: 6" × 38" (15.2cm × 96.5cm) rim; 2" × 11" (5.1cm × 27.9cm) handles

For a large basket, cut: 7" × 45" (17.8cm × 114.3cm) rim; 2" × 12" (5.1cm × 30.5cm) handles

BASKET INSTRUCTIONS

1. After cutting out all of the basket base layers, place them down in the following manner: one Fabric B right side down, batting, heavyweight stabilizer, and the other Fabric A right side up.

2. Place a pin in the top center and the bottom center of the base pieces. Use a different-color straight pin to mark and easily recognize center points.

3. Take the rim panel of Fabric A and place the end ½" (1.3cm) seam allowance over the center pin, and replace the pin to keep this intact.

4. Continue lining up the edge of the rim piece and pin it in place around the edge of the base.

5. Once you have pinned the rim all the way around the base, you will need to connect both ends. Leave another ½" (1.3cm) past the center pin and trim the remainder.

6. Sew the two ½" (1.3cm) seam-allowance ends together, flatten the seams, and pin it down to the center of the base.

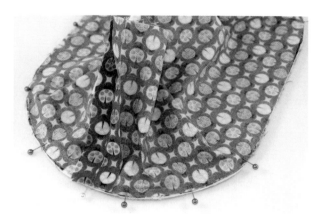

7. Flip the base over and pin the other fabric piece with the batting around the base edge the same way as in steps 3–6. Be sure to open the seam allowance to lay flat and reduce bulk, and avoid bunching up the rim piece on the opposite side while pinning.

8. Sew the perimeter around the basket with a ⅜" (1cm) seam allowance, again making sure not to get the under-side rim bunched into the seam. Flip the basket over and pull the Fabric B and batting rim pieces up and around so now you see all right sides of the rim fabric on the inside and outside. Set aside.

9. To sew the handles, layer 1 piece of batting and 2 pieces of fabric on top, with right sides facing. Then sew along both long edges and turn right side out.

10. Flatten the straps and top stitch both sewn edges.

11. To find the centers on the sides of your basket for handle placement, grab the top and bottom center edges of the rims and spread them apart from each other to flatten the top raw edge. (It will look like the top of the tote bag, and will bring the sides of the rim together.) Line it up to a straightedge and mark your centers on each side with a pin.

12. Pin the handles to the outer side of the rim, to Fabric B and the batting. There is no exact rule on how far apart to place the handle ends; just make sure the handles are spaced the same on both sides.

13. Sew each handle end onto the rim. To make it sturdy and strong to endure child's play, sew a box ¾" (1.9cm) deep with an "X" inside (see step 12 on page 101).

14. Fold down the outer rim (single hem) toward the inside, and fold the inner rim (single hem) toward the inside at the same height. Pin the center sides and ends first. Then pin around the entire rim to prevent shifting.

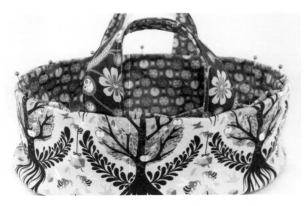

15. Sew a top stitch around the top rim to complete.

CUTTING (FOR PILLOW)

These guidelines include measurements to make a small, medium or large pillow to coordinate with your basket.

For a small 4" × 5½" (10.2cm × 14cm) pillow, cut:

4½" × 6" (11.4cm × 15.2cm) fabric for front

4½" (11.4cm) square backing fabric (cut 2)

3½" × 5" (8.9cm × 12.7cm) batting for pillow insert

For a medium 5" × 7" (12.7cm × 18cm) pillow, cut:

5½" × 7½" (14cm × 19.1cm) fabric for front

5½" (14cm) square backing fabric (cut 2)

4½" × 6½" (11.4cm × 16.5cm) batting for pillow insert

For a large 7½" × 9½" (19.1cm × 24.1cm) pillow, cut:

8" × 10" (20.3cm × 25.4cm) fabric for front

8" (20.3cm) square backing fabric (cut 2)

7" × 9" (17.8cm × 22.9cm) batting for pillow insert

PILLOW INSTRUCTIONS

1. Once the cutting is complete, fold a ⅜" (10mm) double hem on one edge of each backing piece, press and sew it in place.

2. Place the pillow front right side up, and one backing piece right side down. The sewn hem edge should be near the center, but the raw edges align with the top, bottom and sides of the front piece.

3. Place the other back piece right side down on top, with the sewn hem near the center as well as aligned to the opposite side raw edge of the front piece. These back pieces will overlap.

4. Sew all the way around the edge of the pillow, turn right side out and set aside.

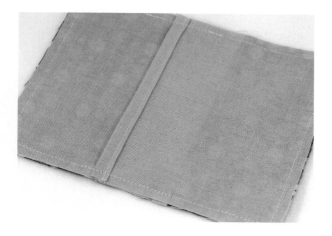

5. Make a pillow insert by folding a piece of batting (or muslin or other fabric) in half and sewing the bottom and side edges (for measurements, see page 96).

6. Stuff the insert and sew the top end closed.

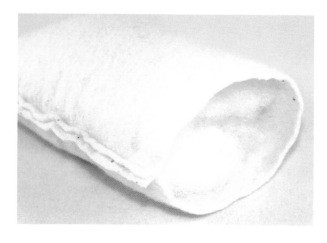

7. Place the pillow insert inside the pillow and pull the other back piece up and over the exposed half to cover.

CUTTING (FOR HOUSE QUILT)

The little house quilt shown above can be made for any size basket. See the layout diagram on page 98 for placement for a 10¾" (27.3cm) square quilt, to go with the smallest basket. Scale up as desired for a 14¾" (37.5cm) or 19¾" (50.2cm) quilt for the medium or large basket. I used multiple fabrics for this blanket so you can clearly see the various pieces. You can use as few or as many different patterns as you'd like.

For a 10¾" (27.3cm) square quilt, cut the following pieces:

Center square (cut 1): 2" (5.1cm)

Roof (cut 1): 1½" × 2" (3.8cm × 5.1cm)

Sky pieces (cut 2): 1" (2.5cm) square

Small side borders (cut 2): 2¾"× 2" (7cm × 5.1cm)

Small top/bottom borders (cut 2): 2" × 5" (5.1cm × 12.7cm)

Large side borders (cut 2): 5" × 3½" (12.7cm × 8.9cm)

Large top/bottom borders (cut 2): 3¼" × 10¾" (8.3cm × 27.3cm)

Batting (cut 1): 10¾" (27.3cm) square

Backing (cut 1): 11¼" (28.6cm) square

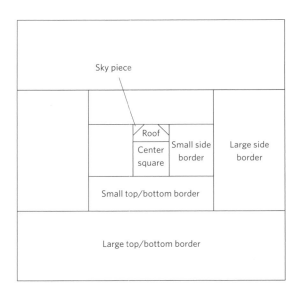

Sky piece

Roof

Center square

Small side border

Large side border

Small top/bottom border

Large top/bottom border

HOUSE QUILT INSTRUCTIONS

1. Sew the roof piece to the house piece with right sides facing.

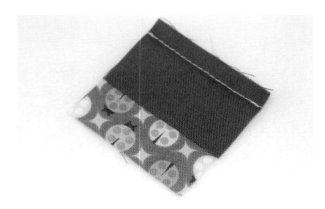

2. Flip up the roof piece, and lay the 2 sky pieces right side down on each corner. Sew the 2 sky pieces to the roof, and then trim the excess corners off.

3. Open up the corners, press and sew the smaller side pieces onto the sides of the house, with right sides together.

4. Flip open the sides and sew the smaller top and bottom pieces on, right sides together. Press this center square and trim if necessary to square it up.

5. Sew the 2 large border sides onto the center house block, with right sides together.

6. Open the sides up and sew the large border top and bottom pieces on with right sides together.

7. To finish the quilt, place the quilt top down right side up, the backing right side down on top, and the batting on top of the wrong side of the backing. Sew all the way around the edge, leaving 2" (5.1cm) open for turning.

8. Trim the corners, turn right side out and then sew a top stitch all the way around. For a simple rolled edge instead of a basic top-stitched edge, follow the instructions on page 15.

Ready, Sew & Go Tote Bag

Ally was working on a beautiful knitted afghan and wanted to show her friend Abby. She shoved her afghan, the colorful balls of yarn she was using and her knitting needles into the nearest plastic bag she could find and headed down the street to Abby's house, whistling as she went. She was so excited to show off her newest project that she didn't notice her bag was getting lighter and lighter.

By the time she got to Abby's, the bag was empty and Ally was devastated. Abby offered to walk with her back down the street to collect everything. They first came upon the balls of yarn and picked them up one by one. They found the beautiful afghan on the sidewalk a few doors down, only a bit unraveled. Near her own home, Ally spotted the needle that had poked through her bag and started it all.

Everyone deserves a quick and beautiful tote bag to carry working projects in. Make one for projects, books, toys, groceries and so much more!

FINISHED SIZE: varies; small (12" [30.5cm] tall) shown on this page, and medium (15" [38.1cm] tall) shown on page 102 (both have a 5" [12.7cm] base)

SUPPLIES

Fabric for lining and outer layer, and low-loft natural batting (unless using pre-quilted outer fabric): ½ yard (.5m) each for child-size tote, ⅝ yard (.6m) each for small tote, ¾ yard (.7m) each for medium tote, or 1 yard (.9m) each for large tote • Thread • Basic sewing tools (pages 8–10)

FABRIC PRINTS SHOWN: from the Hope Chest collection by Josephine Kimberling, courtesy Blend Fabrics/Anna Griffin, Inc.

QUILTING THE FABRIC

If you are using single-faced or double-faced pre-quilted fabric, skip to the cutting section. If you want to pre-quilt your own fabric, do that prior to cutting.

Only the outer side needs to be quilted. If you quilt the lining also, it will be too thick as you sew the base of the bag with this method.

To quilt one side, lay your fabric right side up on top of the low-loft batting. You can follow the fabric pattern or make your own; I followed the stripes in a box pattern. Quilt enough material for the bag and the straps.

CUTTING (FOR BAG BODY)

Below are cutting guidelines for 4 different tote sizes. For the tote bag body, cut 1 each (width × height) for the lining and outer layer.

For a large tote, 15"h (38.1cm) × 22"w (55.9cm) with an 8" (20.3cm) deep base, cut a 24"w × 40"h (61cm × 101.6cm) bag body.

For a medium tote, 12.5"h (31.8cm) × 16"w (40.6cm) with a 5" (12.7cm) deep base, cut an 18"w × 32"h (45.7cm × 81.3cm) bag body.

For a small tote, 9"h (22.9cm) × 12"w (30.5cm) with a 5" (12.7cm) deep base, cut a 14"w × 25"h (35.6cm × 63.5cm) bag body.

For a child-size tote, 7"h (17.8cm) × 8"w (20.3cm) with a 4" (10.2cm) base, cut a 10"w × 20"h (25.4cm × 50.8cm) bag body.

CUTTING (FOR STRAPS)

For the straps, cut 2 each for the lining and outer layer (pre-quilted, either bought or made prior to cutting). The straps can be any length or width you want. I always cut mine 2" (5.1cm) wide and vary the length depending on the size and purpose of the bag—at 25" (63.5cm), as shown on the small tote on page 99; at 20" (50.8cm), as shown on the medium tote on page 102; or at 36" (91.4cm) for a large tote. Strap lengths are mix and match.

INSTRUCTIONS

1. Layer 2 right sides of the strap fabric together (1 lining, 1 quilted outer) and sew the straps lengthwise along both long sides.

2. Turn the straps right side out and top stitch the edges lengthwise along both sides. Set the straps aside.

> *Tip* If you want to add pockets, follow the pocket instructions for the *Adventurer's Backpack* (pages 32–37). Do this prior to sewing the lining and outer pieces together.

3. Take the lining fabric side and fold it in half, with right sides together. Sew a ⅜" (10mm) seam allowance on both side edges from the top, down 3" (7.6cm) only.

4. Take the quilted outer side and repeat step 3, with right sides together, sewing only 3" (7.6cm).

5. Put the lining directly on top of the quilted outer fabric and line up the top, bottom and side edges. Pin in place, starting where the 3" (7.6cm) seams have ended.

6. Lay your tote bag pieces on a ruled mat (or use a straightedge along the sides) so your folded edge is at zero. Push the bottom fold of the lining fabric up in between its own layers to the 5" (12.7cm) mark on your ruled mat. If the fold is at 5" (12.7cm), the 2 new folds that are created are at 2½" (6.4cm) on your ruled mat. This base will be 5" (12.7cm) wide.

7. Now push the bottom fold of the outer fabric up in between its own layers to 5" (12.7cm) also.

8. Pin all the layers together.

9. Sew a ⅜" (1.9cm) seam allowance from the base of the 3" (7.6cm) mark, down to the very end of the folds, on both sides of the bag.

10. Turn the outer layer of the tote bag right side out, leaving the lining on the inside.

11. Find the center of the top raw edge and place the straps at least 5" (12.7cm) apart from each other, 2½" (6.4cm) away from the center mark. You can make this gap wider or narrower based on the size of the bag and length of the straps.

12. Sew ¾" (1.9cm) of the strap onto the outer fabric, making a box and "X" shape inside to provide extra strength.

13. Repeat steps 11–12 to all strap ends.

14. To close the top of the tote bag, flatten the side seams first to reduce bulk. Fold down a single hem 1" (2.5cm) of the quilted outer layer toward the inside of the bag, between the two layers. Fold and pin first at the seams, then in the centers, and then at the base of each strap.

15. Fold down a single hem of the lining 1" (2.5cm) toward the outside of the bag, folding and re-pinning in the same order as step 14.

16. Once both layers are folded in toward each other and pinned together evenly, sew a top stitch (simple or decorative) around the folded edges to complete the tote bag, removing pins as you go.

Tip If you are using a solid fabric for the outer layer of your tote bag and want to add a stripe like on the tote below, you can do so prior to completing step 4 in the main instructions.

1. Place a 2" (5.1cm) strip of fabric facedown, 5" (12.7cm) from the top.

2. Sew the top raw edge of the strip, and then fold upward.

3. Tuck under ¼" (6mm) of the new top raw edge and pin in place.

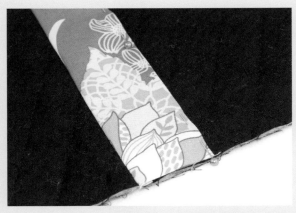

4. Top stitch both the top and the bottom folded edges of the fabric strip.

Repeat all steps to add a stripe on the other end (which will be the other side once sewn together) of the outer fabric, making sure it lines up.

Edie the Lightbulb

Hi! I'm Edie, and I've got a brilliant idea. I've got a lot of ideas, actually. My ideas never stop and keep me awake all night. As soon as I think of one, I try to write it down to get it out of my head, but the next one comes along seconds later. Sometimes it's exhausting, but that's what we lightbulbs do! I can help you think of ideas, too.

Lightbulbs like me come in all different colors and sizes. Even though I'm small, I'm a big helper because I can hold all of your tiny pins and needles. Make me bigger and I'll hold your head while you sleep so you'll have plenty of ideas after a nice long rest.

This was the first three-dimensional pattern I designed while in a college sculpture class. We had to make something from everyday life out of a different material than it would normally be made with, changing its end use. Make a pincushion or enlarge the pattern for a fun pillow.

FINISHED LENGTH: 9" (22.9cm)

SUPPLIES

Templates (page 124) • Fabric: 1 fat quarter (or 2 for variety) for pincushion; yardage for pillow depends on how much you enlarge the pattern (3½ yards [3.2m] if enlarging at 400%) • Muslin (equal amounts) • Stuffing • Thread Basic sewing tools (pages 8–10)

FABRICS SHOWN: from the Freshcut collection by Heather Bailey, courtesy FreeSpirit/Westminster Fibers Fabric

103

INSTRUCTIONS

1. Cut out the lightbulb pattern pieces using the fabric of your choice.

2. Place two bulb top pieces right sides together.

3. Sew along one edge, from the bottom up to the middle of the top.

4. Open these first two pieces and lay a third piece on top of the right panel, right sides together.

5. Sew along the edge, from the bottom up to the middle of the top.

6. Repeat steps 4–5 until all bulb top pieces have been sewn together.

7. With right sides still together, take the first bulb piece and the last bulb piece and sew along the edge, from the bottom about ½" (1.3cm) up. Leave 1" to 2" (2.5cm to 5.1cm) open for turning and stuffing, and then sew the remainder up to the top.

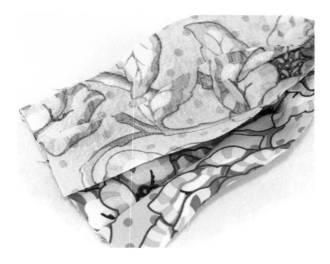

8. Turn the bulb top right side out temporarily and set aside.

9. Lay one screw base fabric piece on top of a screw base muslin piece. Using a fabric marking pen and the pattern guide or ruler, mark the two diagonal lines onto the fabric.

Tip Mark the diagonal lines on the muslin side to avoid having to clean the ink off. I'm showing the pretty fabric side for the pictures.

10. Sew one of the diagonal lines using a simple stitch.

11. Lightly stuff the diagonal space in between the two stitch lines, and pin in place along the second unstitched line. This will be the raised "thread" of the screw base piece. If you overstuff, it will cause the fabric to pucker.

17. Line up the raw edges of the bulb top with the finished screw base piece and pin all the way around the raw edge.

12. Once pinned all the way across, sew the second line with a simple stitch.

13. Repeat steps 9–12 to make the other half of the screw base.

14. Place both screw base halves right sides together and sew both panels together on the shorter end.

15. Fold both panels together with right sides facing, and sew the other short end together.

16. Place the finished screw base wrong side out onto the end of the bulb top (which is currently right side out) so right sides are facing.

18. Sew these two pieces together, all the way around the raw edge.

19. Turn the entire bulb wrong side out and set aside.

20. To make the electrical contact end piece, take the electric contact pattern and lay it on top of a round piece of muslin. Using a marking pen and the pattern guide, mark the smaller circle onto the fabric in the center. (I would again recommend marking the muslin side.)

21. Sew the smaller circle with a simple stitch, three-quarters of the way around.

22. Lightly stuff the circle and sew it closed. Again, if you overstuff, it will cause the fabric to pucker.

23. With the lightbulb wrong side out, pin the electric contact piece to the end of the screw base.

24. Sew all the way around the raw edge to connect these two final pieces.

25. Clip or notch all curved edges, being careful not to clip the seams.

26. Turn the entire lightbulb right side out and stuff to the desired firmness.

Tip You can make the bulb a true pincushion that will keep your pins and needles sharpened by stuffing it with walnut shells, sand-blasting glass beads or emery sand.

27. Sew the opening closed with a ladder stitch.

The Travelers: HAPPY & KITTY

Howdy! I am Happy the Trailer, and this is Kitty the Station Wagon. We've been traveling all over the country, seeing the sights and having a blast. This past summer, we were cruising through California and Utah. We didn't stay long before heading back to Texas, the place we call home. We stop here in between our trips and just love those cowboys and corn dogs at the rodeos!

Although we enjoy stopping home for a spell, it's high time we start heading east to see the trees turning all sorts of colors. I hear it's real pretty this time of year. But it doesn't last long before the snow starts to fall, so we best get going soon. So what do you say? Wanna join us? We'd love some company. But y'all better love singin' songs, campin' under the stars and roastin' marshmellahs!

Don't be surprised if, while making your own vintage trailer and station wagon, memories surface of the good ol' days traveling in the family Ford with a Shasta in tow.

FINISHED LENGTH: 7" (17.8cm) trailer, 6" (15.2cm) station wagon

SUPPLIES

Templates (page 124) • Fabric: 1 fat quarter, or 2 for variety (will make 2 trailers or 2 wagons, or 1 of each); 3" (7.6cm) wide strip at least 20" (51cm) long • Scrap of heavy-weight stabilizer (for trailer only) • Scraps of clear vinyl • Stuffing • Buttons: 2 tiny, 1 ball-shaped and (3) ¾" (1.9cm) fabric-covered for trailer; 2 tiny and 4 regular or fabric-covered for wagon • Thread • Scrap of decorative string for wagon hitch • Basic sewing tools (pages 8–10)

TRAILER INSTRUCTIONS

1. Cut out the trailer pattern pieces using the fabric of your choice. The sides of the trailer can be made from a single piece of fabric or pieced together. You can sew 2 fabrics right sides together and then cut out the side pieces at any angle or straight across.

2. To make a door, place 2 door pieces of fabric right sides together. If you have made your trailer side with more than one piece of fabric (as pictured), make sure the seam on the door will match up to the seam on the trailer once finished.

3. Sew the door pieces right sides together, leaving a small opening on the side for turning and to sew into the seam.

4. Notch the top curved edge of the door and turn right side out.

5. Lay the finished door facedown on the right side of the trailer piece (looks like the door is open), lining it up and leaving enough room for the bottom seam allowance.

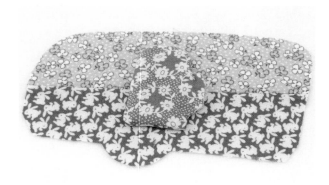

6. Take the last door fabric piece and draw the doorway frame and the door opening on the wrong side with a fabric marker.

7. Place this doorway piece (do not cut out the door frame or opening yet) right sides together on top of the trailer side, so that the raw edge of the door will be sewn into the doorway opening seam.

8. Sew this piece down by sewing all the way around the doorway opening on the line drawn in step 6.

9. Draw a smaller doorway hole ¼" (6mm) away from the seam sewn in the previous step and carefully cut a hole directly in the center, and then on the new line.

10. Clip the inside seam allowance and be sure to clip the two bottom corners. Get as close to the seam as you can without clipping the seam itself.

Tip Although the image shows the doorway frame cut out (for clear placement purposes), I would recommend not trimming this outer edge until after steps 11–14 are completed.

11. Flip over the entire trailer side piece, and once the frame is turned inward, press the frame on the inside.

12. Cut a piece of the vinyl and place it in the doorway on the wrong side of the trailer piece.

13. Try fussy cutting a figure for inside the doorway. Place it right side down on top of the vinyl piece, and pin in place. Flip over the entire trailer side piece.

14. Top stitch around the entire doorway to attach the vinyl and fabric.

15. Trim the outer edge of the doorway frame, fabric and any excess vinyl.

16. With the door done, follow steps 6–15 using the window templates to make the windows for both trailer side pieces. Then set these pieces aside.

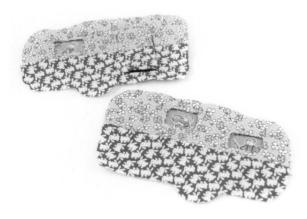

17. Before adding a front window (a back window too, if you choose), prep your 3" (7.6cm) wide strip of fabric. If you used more than one piece of fabric on the sides, be sure to cut and sew the appropriate pieces so your fabrics will match up to the seams on this center piece, as was done for the door. Follow steps 6–12 to make the front window opening and place the vinyl.

18. You can use a fussy-cut image or make the front or back windows look like a curtain is inside. Take a larger piece of fabric and run a gathering stitch just above the top and just below the bottom of the window opening, and pin in place.

19. Flip the pieces right side up. Top stitch around the window opening. Flip these pieces right side down and trim any excess window, curtain and vinyl pieces.

20. Sew 2 sides of the hitch pieces right sides together, with the heavyweight stabilizer on top and trim off the pointed tip.

21. Turn these pieces right side out and sew the raw edge of the hitch to the end of the 3" (7.6cm) center strip piece.

22. Pin the 3" (7.6cm) wide strip of fabric all the way around both of the trailer edges, so that the hitch piece is positioned in the front on the bottom of the trailer and all right sides are facing inward. Be sure your strip matches up to the seams on the sides of the trailer.

109

23. Sew the strip to the sides, removing pins as you go, and trim the end of the strip accordingly. Tuck the hitch inside.

24. Sew the beginning of the strip piece to the end of the strip only on the outer corners. Leave the center open for turning and stuffing.

25. Carefully notch all the curved edges without clipping the seams.

26. Turn the trailer right side out, stuff to the desired firmness, and close the opening underneath the hitch with a ladder stitch.

27. Add one "spare tire" fabric button to the rear of the trailer and two fabric buttons for side wheels.

28. Add 2 tiny buttons for door handles and a ball button to represent the hitch. If desired, you can wrap a small piece of thread around the door buttons to hold it closed (not shown).

WAGON INSTRUCTIONS

The station wagon instructions are very similar to the trailer. You can make the wagon as simple or as detailed as you'd like, by piecing certain patterns and solids together as I have done on the sides (to add a stripe) and on the roof (for an old-school look), and then cutting out your pattern pieces.

To make your wagon, follow these steps as you reference the trailer instructions.

1. Follow trailer step 1.

2. After you have cut out your pattern pieces, skip trailer steps 2–5, as there are no door panels on the wagon. Follow trailer steps 6–15 to make each of the side windows and then both of the front and back windows. The seam allowance is very small on the windows of the wagon. Be careful not to enlarge the window size beyond the actual pattern size.

3. Unless you want to make the back window look like it has curtains also, skip trailer steps 17–21.

4. Pin the 3" (7.6cm) wide strip of fabric all the way around both of the wagon sides, as you did for the trailer in step 22. However, for the wagon, you will start and stop the strip so it is positioned in the back of the wagon at the bumper. All right sides should be facing inward.

5. Continue following trailer steps 23–25. Turn the wagon right side out, stuff to the desired firmness, and close the opening on the bumper with a ladder stitch. Place a little loop of decorative string in the center of the bumper so you can attach the wagon to the trailer hitch.

6. As you did for the trailer, add buttons for the wheels and doors. The wagon will need 4 regular or fabric-covered buttons for the tires (smaller than the ones used on the trailer). The tiny buttons that were used on the trailer door can also be used on the wagon doors.

Templates

THE GNOMES

Shown at 50%; enlarge at 200%.
Cutting instructions are per doll.

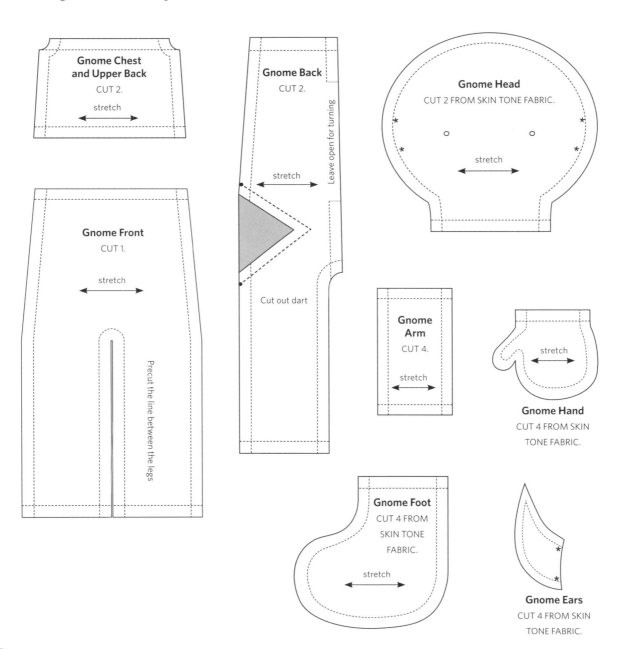

Gnome Chest and Upper Back
CUT 2.
stretch

Gnome Front
CUT 1.
stretch

Precut the line between the legs

Gnome Back
CUT 2.
stretch
Leave open for turning
Cut out dart

Gnome Head
CUT 2 FROM SKIN TONE FABRIC.
stretch

Gnome Arm
CUT 4.
stretch

Gnome Hand
CUT 4 FROM SKIN TONE FABRIC.
stretch

Gnome Foot
CUT 4 FROM SKIN TONE FABRIC.
stretch

Gnome Ears
CUT 4 FROM SKIN TONE FABRIC.

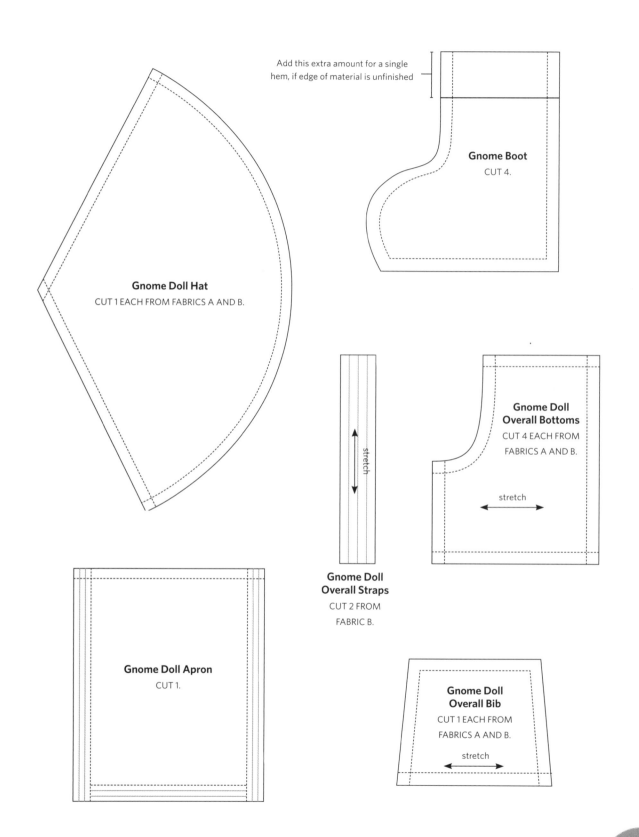

Add this extra amount for a single
hem, if edge of material is unfinished

Gnome Boot
CUT 4.

Gnome Doll Hat
CUT 1 EACH FROM FABRICS A AND B.

stretch

**Gnome Doll
Overall Bottoms**
CUT 4 EACH FROM
FABRICS A AND B.

stretch

**Gnome Doll
Overall Straps**
CUT 2 FROM
FABRIC B.

Gnome Doll Apron
CUT 1.

**Gnome Doll
Overall Bib**
CUT 1 EACH FROM
FABRICS A AND B.

stretch

ADVENTURER'S BACKPACK

Shown at 50%; enlarge at 200%.

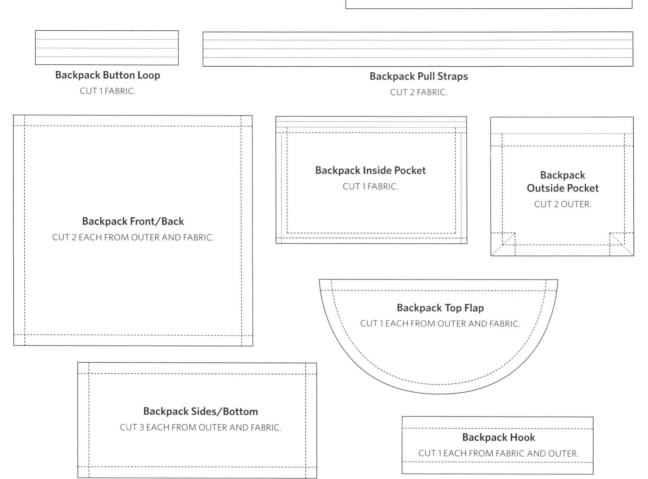

Backpack Straps
CUT 2 EACH FROM OUTER AND LINING.

Backpack Button Loop
CUT 1 FABRIC.

Backpack Pull Straps
CUT 2 FABRIC.

Backpack Front/Back
CUT 2 EACH FROM OUTER AND FABRIC.

Backpack Inside Pocket
CUT 1 FABRIC.

Backpack Outside Pocket
CUT 2 OUTER.

Backpack Top Flap
CUT 1 EACH FROM OUTER AND FABRIC.

Backpack Sides/Bottom
CUT 3 EACH FROM OUTER AND FABRIC.

Backpack Hook
CUT 1 EACH FROM FABRIC AND OUTER.

MOUSE PALS: SHERBET AND PISTACHIO

Shown at 50%; enlarge at 200%.

Mouse Tail
CUT 2.

stretch

Mouse Body
CUT 2.
stretch

Precut on solid line
Mouse Head
CUT 2.
stretch

Mouse Arms
CUT 4.

stretch
Mouse Legs
CUT 4.

Mouse Ears
CUT 4.

MAGICAL MUSHROOMS

Shown at 50%; enlarge at 200%.

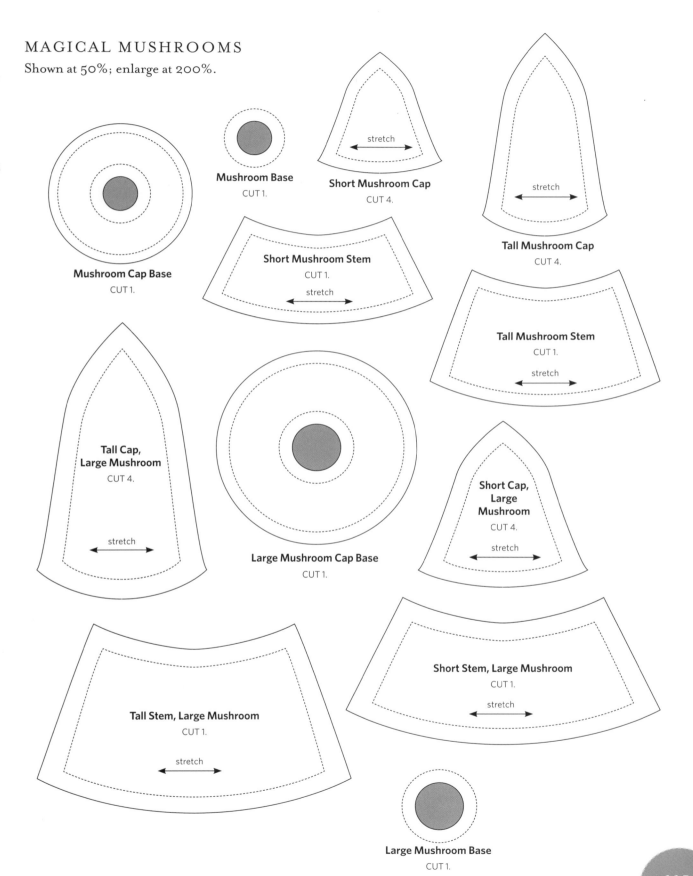

Mushroom Base
CUT 1.

Short Mushroom Cap
CUT 4.

stretch

Tall Mushroom Cap
CUT 4.

stretch

Mushroom Cap Base
CUT 1.

Short Mushroom Stem
CUT 1.

stretch

Tall Mushroom Stem
CUT 1.

stretch

**Tall Cap,
Large Mushroom**
CUT 4.

stretch

Large Mushroom Cap Base
CUT 1.

**Short Cap,
Large
Mushroom**
CUT 4.

stretch

Tall Stem, Large Mushroom
CUT 1.

stretch

Short Stem, Large Mushroom
CUT 1.

stretch

Large Mushroom Base
CUT 1.

MORTON THE PAINTED TURTLE

Shown at 50%; enlarge at 200%.

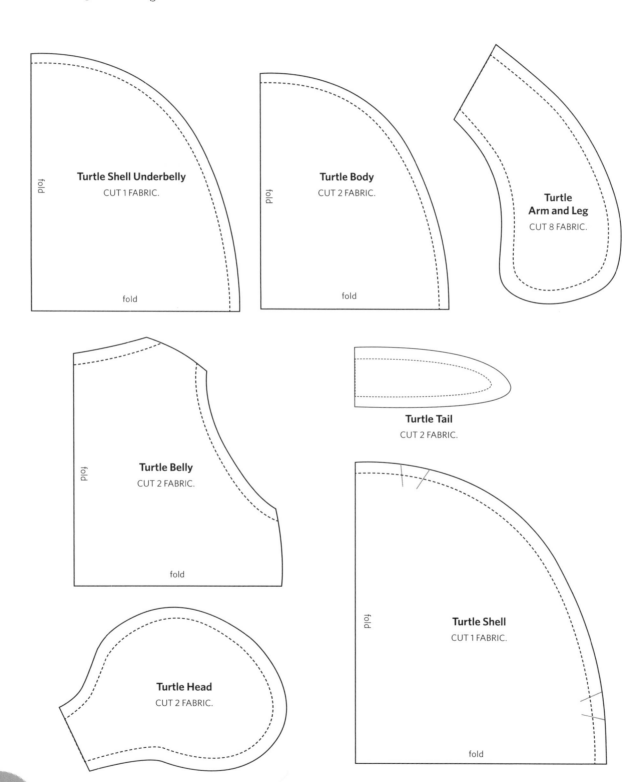

Turtle Shell Underbelly
CUT 1 FABRIC.
fold

Turtle Body
CUT 2 FABRIC.
fold

Turtle
Arm and Leg
CUT 8 FABRIC.

Turtle Belly
CUT 2 FABRIC.
fold

Turtle Tail
CUT 2 FABRIC.

Turtle Head
CUT 2 FABRIC.

Turtle Shell
CUT 1 FABRIC.
fold

WATER BABY THE ROWBOAT

Shown at 50%; enlarge at 200%.

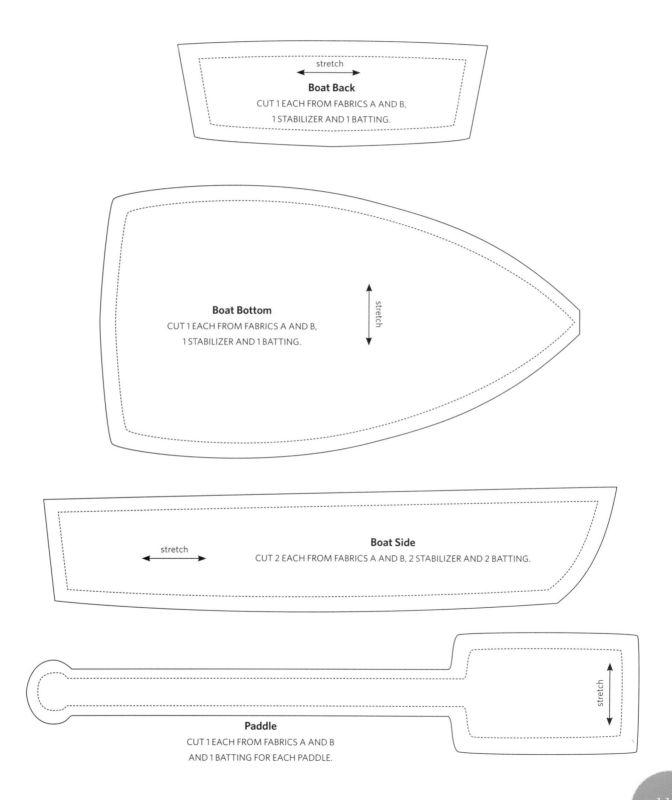

Boat Back
CUT 1 EACH FROM FABRICS A AND B,
1 STABILIZER AND 1 BATTING.

stretch

Boat Bottom
CUT 1 EACH FROM FABRICS A AND B,
1 STABILIZER AND 1 BATTING.

stretch

Boat Side
CUT 2 EACH FROM FABRICS A AND B, 2 STABILIZER AND 2 BATTING.

stretch

Paddle
CUT 1 EACH FROM FABRICS A AND B
AND 1 BATTING FOR EACH PADDLE.

stretch

PINCHY THE LOBSTER

Shown at 50%; enlarge at 200%.

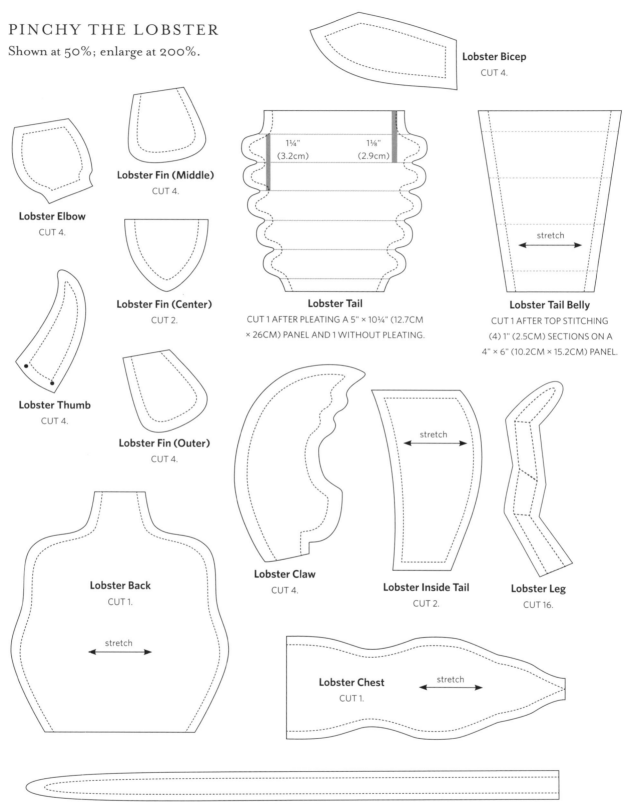

Lobster Bicep
CUT 4.

Lobster Elbow
CUT 4.

Lobster Fin (Middle)
CUT 4.

Lobster Fin (Center)
CUT 2.

Lobster Thumb
CUT 4.

Lobster Fin (Outer)
CUT 4.

1¼"
(3.2cm)

1⅛"
(2.9cm)

Lobster Tail
CUT 1 AFTER PLEATING A 5" × 10¼" (12.7CM × 26CM) PANEL AND 1 WITHOUT PLEATING.

stretch

Lobster Tail Belly
CUT 1 AFTER TOP STITCHING (4) 1" (2.5CM) SECTIONS ON A 4" × 6" (10.2CM × 15.2CM) PANEL.

Lobster Claw
CUT 4.

stretch

Lobster Inside Tail
CUT 2.

Lobster Leg
CUT 16.

Lobster Back
CUT 1.

stretch

Lobster Chest
CUT 1.

stretch

Lobster Antenna
CUT 4.

BOB THE BUOY

Shown at 50%; enlarge at 200%.

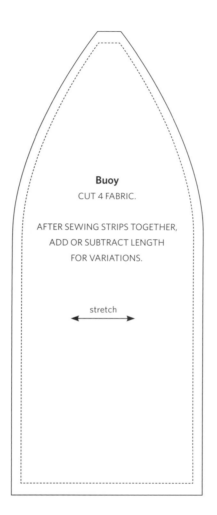

Buoy

CUT 4 FABRIC.

AFTER SEWING STRIPS TOGETHER,
ADD OR SUBTRACT LENGTH
FOR VARIATIONS.

stretch

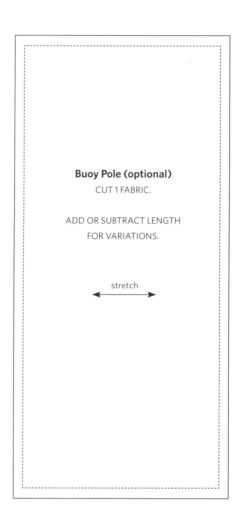

Buoy Pole (optional)

CUT 1 FABRIC.

ADD OR SUBTRACT LENGTH
FOR VARIATIONS.

stretch

Buoy Base

CUT 1 FABRIC.

cut out center if adding pole

Buoy Pole Tip

CUT 1 FABRIC.

CASCO THE DOLPHIN (WITH MAMA)

Shown at 50%; enlarge at 200%.

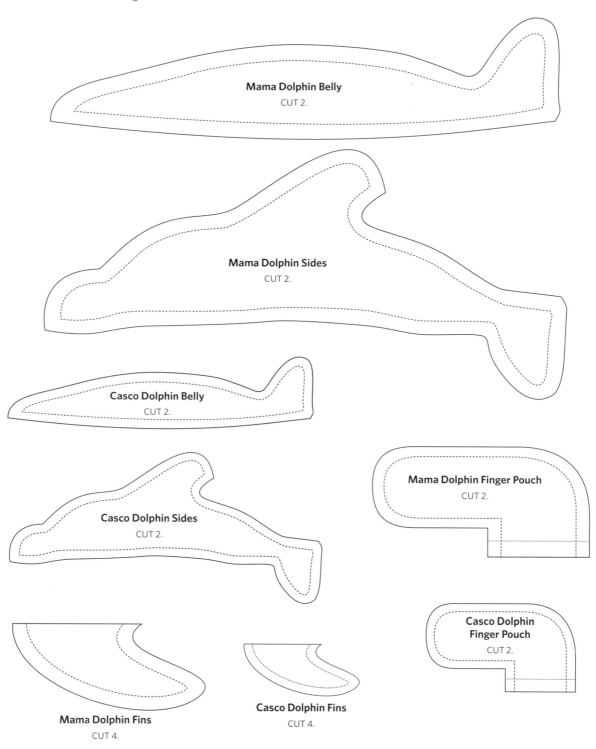

Mama Dolphin Belly
CUT 2.

Mama Dolphin Sides
CUT 2.

Casco Dolphin Belly
CUT 2.

Casco Dolphin Sides
CUT 2.

Mama Dolphin Finger Pouch
CUT 2.

**Casco Dolphin
Finger Pouch**
CUT 2.

Mama Dolphin Fins
CUT 4.

Casco Dolphin Fins
CUT 4.

BEAR BUDDIES: SNOWFLAKE AND ANGEL

Shown at 50%; enlarge at 200%.

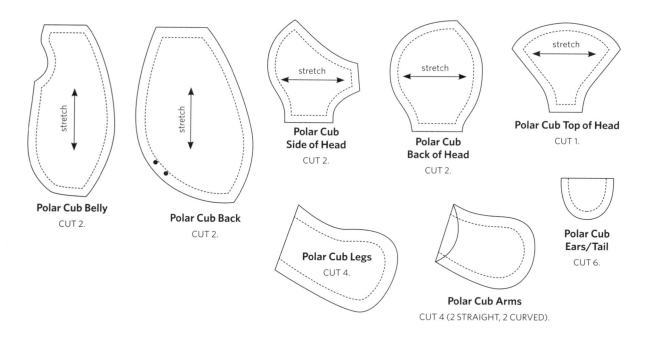

Polar Cub Belly
CUT 2.

Polar Cub Back
CUT 2.

**Polar Cub
Side of Head**
CUT 2.

**Polar Cub
Back of Head**
CUT 2.

Polar Cub Top of Head
CUT 1.

Polar Cub Legs
CUT 4.

Polar Cub Arms
CUT 4 (2 STRAIGHT, 2 CURVED).

**Polar Cub
Ears/Tail**
CUT 6.

DRIFTER THE ORCA WHALE

Shown at 50%; enlarge at 200%.

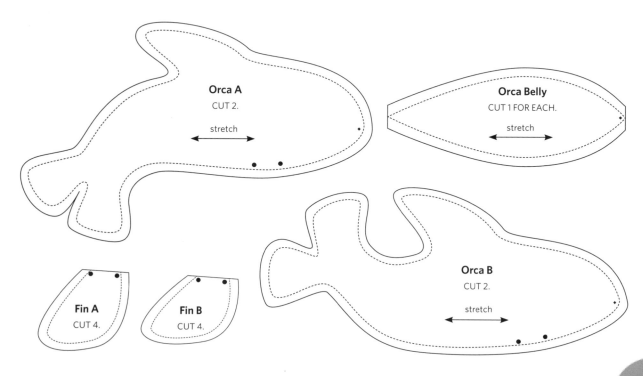

Orca A
CUT 2.
stretch

Orca Belly
CUT 1 FOR EACH.
stretch

Fin A
CUT 4.

Fin B
CUT 4.

Orca B
CUT 2.
stretch

BOOBOO THE IGLOO

Shown at 50%; enlarge at 200%.

Igloo Pole Base Ends

CUT 6.

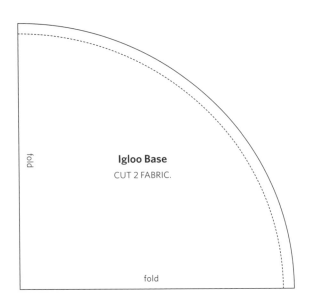

Igloo Base

CUT 2 FABRIC.

fold

fold

Igloo Doorway Base

CUT 1 EACH FROM
FABRICS A AND B AND
1 MEDIUM-WEIGHT STABILIZER.

stretch

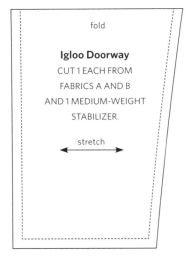

fold

Igloo Doorway

CUT 1 EACH FROM
FABRICS A AND B
AND 1 MEDIUM-WEIGHT
STABILIZER.

stretch

stretch

placement for
igloo pole tabs

Igloo Panels

CUT 6 EACH FROM FABRICS A AND B.

CUT 2 DOORWAY OPENINGS
ON 1 OF EACH FABRIC A AND B PANEL.

placement for
igloo pole tabs

placement
for igloo pole
base ends

**Igloo
Pole Tabs**

CUT 24.

MIMI THE HOT-AIR BALLOON

Shown at 50%; enlarge at 200%.

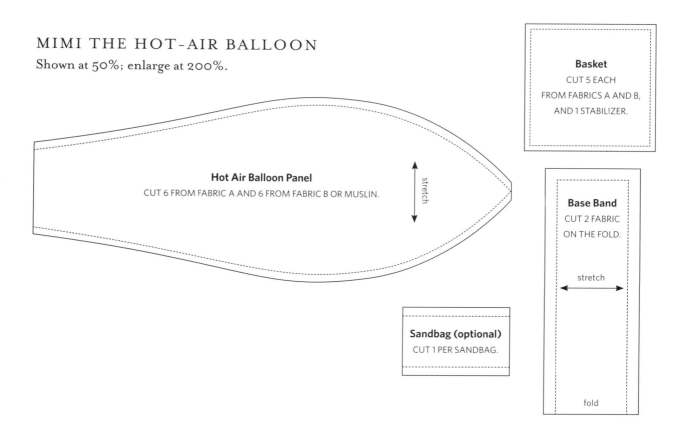

Basket
CUT 5 EACH
FROM FABRICS A AND B,
AND 1 STABILIZER.

Hot Air Balloon Panel
CUT 6 FROM FABRIC A AND 6 FROM FABRIC B OR MUSLIN.

stretch

Base Band
CUT 2 FABRIC
ON THE FOLD.

stretch

fold

Sandbag (optional)
CUT 1 PER SANDBAG.

DOLLY MOSES BASKET

Shown at 50%; enlarge at 200%.

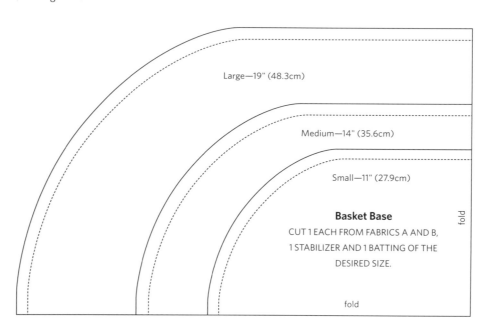

Large—19" (48.3cm)

Medium—14" (35.6cm)

Small—11" (27.9cm)

Basket Base
CUT 1 EACH FROM FABRICS A AND B,
1 STABILIZER AND 1 BATTING OF THE
DESIRED SIZE.

fold

fold

EDIE THE LIGHTBULB

Shown at 50%; enlarge at 200% for pincushion, or 400% for pillow.

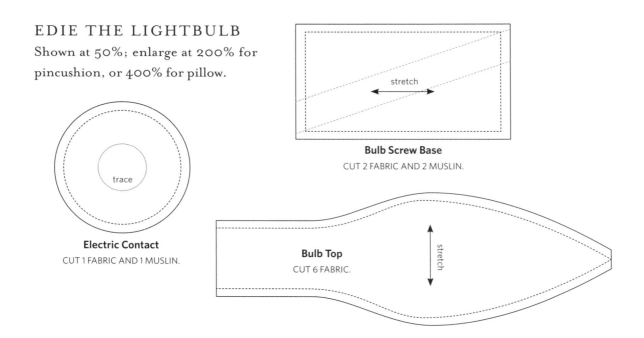

Bulb Screw Base

CUT 2 FABRIC AND 2 MUSLIN.

trace

Electric Contact

CUT 1 FABRIC AND 1 MUSLIN.

stretch

Bulb Top

CUT 6 FABRIC.

THE TRAVELERS: HAPPY AND KITTY

Shown at 50%; enlarge at 200%.

stretch

Trailer Side

CUT 2 FABRIC.

Trailer Hitch

CUT 2 FABRIC
AND 1 HEAVYWEIGHT STABILIZER.

Trailer Back Window

CUT 1 FABRIC.

Trailer Side Window

CUT 1 FABRIC EACH.

Wagon Side Window 1

CUT 2 FABRIC.

Wagon Side

CUT 2 FABRIC.

stretch

Trailer Door

CUT 3 FABRIC.

Wagon Back Windshield

CUT 1 FABRIC.

Wagon Front Windshield

CUT 1 FABRIC.

Wagon Side Window 2

CUT 2 FABRIC.

INDEX

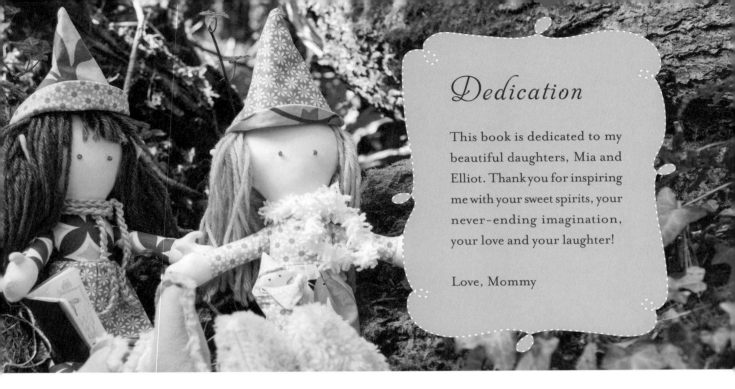

Dedication

This book is dedicated to my beautiful daughters, Mia and Elliot. Thank you for inspiring me with your sweet spirits, your never-ending imagination, your love and your laughter!

Love, Mommy

17 16 15 14 13   5 4 3 2 1

DISTRIBUTED IN CANADA BY FRASER DIRECT
100 Armstrong Avenue
Georgetown, ON, Canada L7G 5S4
Tel: (905) 877-4411

DISTRIBUTED IN THE U.K. AND EUROPE BY F+W MEDIA INTERNATIONAL
Brunel House, Newton Abbot, Devon, TQ12 4PU, England
Tel: (+44) 1626 323200, Fax: (+44) 1626 323319
Email: postmaster@davidandcharles.co.uk

DISTRIBUTED IN AUSTRALIA BY CAPRICORN LINK
P.O. Box 704, S. Windsor NSW, 2756 Australia
Tel: (02) 4560-1600, Fax: (02) 4577 5288
Email: books@capricornlink.com.au

ISBN-13: 978-1-4402-3519-1
ISBN-10: 1-4402-3519-8
SRN: U2257

www.fwmedia.com

Edited by *Stefanie Laufersweiler* and *Roseann Biederman*

Designed by *Julie Barnett*

Production coordinated by *Greg Nock*

Step photography by *Kerry Goulder*

Location photography by *Bangwallop Photography* except for photographs on pages 6, 76 and 81 by *Nadra Edgerley*

METRIC CONVERSION CHART

to convert	to	multiply by
inches	centimeters	2.54
centimeters	inches	0.4
feet	centimeters	30.5
centimeters	feet	0.03
yards	meters	0.9
meters	yards	1.1

Projects have been designed and created using imperial measurements and, although metric measurements have been provided, it is important to stick to using either imperial or metric throughout as discrepancies can occur.

About the author

Photo by Nadra Edgerley

Kerry Goulder's sewing patterns and crafts have been featured on the covers and pages of *Crafts 'n Things* magazine, as well as *STUFFED* magazine. She has also designed five sewing patterns for Anna Griffin, Inc. that debuted at the May 2011 International Quilt Market.

Being born in Texas and having lived there and in Long Island, New York, has given Kerry a love of horses, sunshine, the smell of salt in the air and the feeling of sand in her toes. In 1994, she met her husband in a sculpture class while studying fine arts at the University of Hartford in Connecticut. Kerry and her husband, Travis, have settled in a beautiful coastal Maine town with their two daughters.

When she's not sewing, Kerry enjoys dance parties in the kitchen with her daughters, date nights with her husband, and talking on the phone regularly with her twin sister, Sue, conjuring up new ideas. Visit Kerry's website at www.kidgiddy.com.

ACKNOWLEDGMENTS

Without the following people and companies, this book would cease to exist.

First and foremost, I need to thank my Heavenly Father for carrying me through this process and blessing me with my amazing family and a fun talent to share. To my best friend and husband, Travis, for his love, patience and endless support with all the housework when I was mentally spent and our house was trashed. To my girls, for all the cuddles, kisses and encouraging words.

Thank you to my mom, Karen, and my twin sister, Sue, for being my creative sounding boards and so much more. To Granny, for teaching my mom everything she has taught me. To Amy for being my spiritual buoy, to Danna for giving me my first (creative workhorse) sewing machine, to Nadra for making me feel so beautiful, to Phoebe for encouraging me to submit my first publication, and to all my friends and family who have supported me through the years.

Thank you to Anna Griffin for giving me a running start straight out of the gate, and opening doors for me. A special thanks to Rachel Scheller for seeing something in my work and style worthy of a book, and all the folks at F+W: Vanessa, Stef, Julie and Roseann—you've now seen the best and the worst of me. Thank you for breathing life into my book.

Heather Bailey, words cannot express my gratitude to you, for your willingness to help others like me grow! Thank you for writing the foreword for my book.

I'd like to thank the following companies for providing the gorgeous fabrics and necessary materials: Bosal Foam & Fiber, Blend Fabrics by Anna Griffin, Inc., Michael Miller Fabrics, Westminster Fibers Fabric (Rowan/FreeSpirit), Windham Fabrics and Kreinik Mfg. Co., Inc. threads.

Last but not least, I'd like to thank you. The one holding my book, reading it, considering it, buying it, sharing it, appreciating it, and creating your own stories to pass on. I can't thank you enough, but I will try.

Fabric you love, supplies you need, books that inspire...

You'll find everything you need to start and complete a successful sewing project—and you don't even have to leave the house! Visit store.MarthaPullen.com for all the fabrics, threads, tools and notions you need, and check out these exciting titles for valuable instruction and endless inspiration.

visit store.marthapullen.com

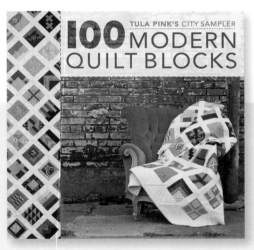

Tula Pink's City Sampler: 100 Modern Quilt Blocks
Tula Pink

Create a sampler quilt as unique as you are! Tula Pink gives you an inspiring quilt block collection. Make a beautiful, modern quilt of your own design with the 100 original quilt blocks inside, or try one of five city-themed sampler quilts designed by Tula.

The Sewing Machine Classroom
Learning the ins and outs of your machine
Charlene Phillips

Learn all about your new best friend—your sewing machine! From fabric to feet to finished product, you'll be guided through techniques for mastering your machine and using it to perform basic to advanced stitching tasks. Whether you've been sewing for years or just gotten the itch, you'll find invaluable information inside for using your machine to its maximum potential.